TALKING GOD

ALSO BY GARY GUTTING

What Philosophy Can Do

Thinking the Impossible: French Philosophy Since 1960

What Philosophers Know:
Case Studies in Recent Analytic Philosophy

Foucault: A Very Short Introduction

French Philosophy in the Twentieth Century

Pragmatic Liberalism and the Critique of Modernity

Michel Foucault's Archaeology of Scientific Reason

Religious Belief and Religious Skepticism

TALKING GOD

Philosophers on Belief

Gary Gutting

W. W. NORTON & COMPANY
Independent Publishers Since 1923
NEW YORK   LONDON

All interviews originally appeared in *The Stone* column of the *New York Times*.

For information about permission to reproduce selections from this book,
write to Permissions, W. W. Norton & Company, Inc.,
500 Fifth Avenue, New York, NY 10110

For information about special discounts for bulk purchases, please contact
W. W. Norton Special Sales at specialsales@wwnorton.com or 800-233-4830

Manufacturing by Helene Berinsky
Book design by Quad Graphics
Production manager: Lauren Abbate

ISBN 978-0-393-35281-8 (pbk.)

W. W. Norton & Company, Inc.
500 Fifth Avenue, New York, N.Y. 10110
www.wwnorton.com

W. W. Norton & Company Ltd.
15 Carlisle Street, London W1D 3BS

1 2 3 4 5 6 7 8 9 0

To Anastasia

For so many fascinating conversations

Contents

PREFACE

Some people say religion has nothing important to teach us; it's just a residue of long-discredited ways of thinking and acting. I'm open to that possibility but think it's more likely that religion—like art, music, and science—deserves the central place it has long held in human culture. I don't, however, assume that we have an adequate understanding of how and why religion is important. In particular, I suspect that many religious believers don't have an adequate understanding of the real truth of their religion. Philosophical and scientific critiques may well undermine the "self-understanding" of various religions. But it doesn't follow that there's not a truth in religion that believers themselves do not (at least explicitly) grasp. My goal in this series of interviews with philosophers on religion was to see what this truth, if any, might be.

Here I present, essentially unchanged, the twelve interviews that appeared during 2014 in *The Stone*, the *New York Times* philosophy blog. I conducted each interview by email, with the final version approved by the interviewee. The interviews make up about half of this volume. I've added introductions to each interview, providing some background and context, as well as further comments at the end, giving my own take on issues raised in each interview. A "self-interview" (which concluded the *Times* series) offers my personal reaction to the interviews and my resulting overall view of religion.

The interviews cover many of the main issues that concern philosophers interested in religion, but I've emphasized the distinctive views of my interlocutors over a more systematic and complete account. There is, however, a logical progression in the order of interviews. We begin with general defenses of theism (Alvin Plantinga) and of atheism (Louise Antony), and then move to two more specific defenses of religion (John Caputo's Christianity à la Derrida and Howard Wettstein's Jewish experience). Next, there is Philip Kitcher's nuanced but powerful "soft atheism", followed by Tim Maudlin's deployment of scientific cosmology against traditional religious claims, and Michael Ruse's sympathetic but ultimately atheistic reflections on religion and evolution. Then we move the discussion beyond Judaism and Christianity, as I talk with Sajjad Rizvi on Islam, Jonardon Ganeri on Hinduism, and Jay Garfield on Buddhism. Finally, there is a discussion with Keith DeRose on the rationality of both theism and atheism, a historical perspective from Daniel Garber, and my "self-interview". Readers may find this overall structure helpful, but each of the interviews can stand on its own, and they can be read in any order.

My own training and interests—not to mention the focus of *The Stone*—explains why in these interviews "talking God" means primarily "talking philosophy". Other disciplines, such as psychology, anthropology, sociology, history, biology, and neuroscience, also offer fruitful paths to understanding religion. But religions offer answers to fundamental questions about human existence that require the intellectual tools philosophers have developed over the centuries. There are those who argue that only scientists (if anyone) can answer these fundamental questions. But their arguments require them to grapple with philosophical questions about what there is (metaphysics), how we can know it (epistemology), and what follows about how we should live (ethics).

Others will insist that religion is a matter of emotion rather than reason: "the heart", as Pascal said, "has its reasons, which reason can never know". But we are never entirely rational or entirely emotional, and the two are inevitably combined in our lives. We will question a rational conclusion that just doesn't feel right but also be uneasy with an emotional commitment that we suspect makes no rational sense. Even Pascal in his *Pensées* offered an elaborate argument for the truth of Christianity. His famous wager argument (of which we will hear more later) was just his last desperate effort to lead the nonbeliever to God. Religion does not reduce to philosophy, but any mature faith will have some sort of rational underpinnings that are open to philosophical reflection. These conversations are contributions to that reflection.

I have tried to represent a wide range of views on religion, both positive and negative. There is a particular emphasis on the God of Christian theism as the inevitable starting point in a Western culture formed and still strongly influenced by Christian thinking. But there are also discussions of Jewish, Muslim, Hindu, and Buddhist perspectives, which raise serious questions about Christian presuppositions and suggest alternative religious paths. Almost half the interviews are with philosophers who identify as atheists. This is appropriate both because a good majority of professional philosophers are atheists and because the major concern of contemporary philosophy of religion has been whether there is any defensible basis for believing in God. Readers will, however, see various forms of atheism that are considerably more nuanced than the atheism of popular polemics.

My goal in this volume is not to change minds but to advance lines of thought that readers—no matter what their views on religion—can engage with in their own ways and for their own purposes. My hope it that this sample of philosophers "talking God" will lead readers to their own fruitful conversations.

My thanks to the philosophers I interviewed for the clarity, intelligence, and honesty of their responses and for their cooperation in putting together this volume. Thanks also to Peter Catapano and Jamie Ryerson at the *New York Times* for their expert editing of the interviews, and at Norton to Brendan Curry for encouraging the project, to Sophie Duvernoy for many editorial improvements, and to Nathaniel Dennett for excellent help with the last stages of the publication process. Thanks, finally, to the exceptional Norton production team, including Lauren Abbate, Nancy Palmquist, Susan Sanfrey, and copyeditor Rachelle Mandik.

TALKING GOD

1

A Case for Theism

(Alvin Plantinga)

Although most philosophers today are highly skeptical of religion, there are some strong voices in favor of belief. This is primarily due to Alvin Plantinga, who, since the 1960s, has developed philosophy of religion into an area where philosophical believers, especially Christians, are able to defend and elaborate upon their faith. Plantinga's work gained serious attention, even among those who rejected his religious positions, because of his important contributions to mainstream metaphysics and epistemology. He initially responded to two major challenges to religious belief: the alleged lack of good arguments for the existence of a divine being, and the problem of evil in the world.

In 1974, Plantinga made quite a splash with his rehabilitation of the ontological argument, Saint Anselm's effort to show that God's existence follows logically from his nature as a supremely perfect being. Plantinga crafted an ingenious argument purporting to prove that, if God's existence is possible, it is also necessary. As we see in the interview, he is also favorably disposed to many other standard theistic arguments, particularly the recent "fine-tuning" argument based on the cosmology of the Big Bang. But Plantinga's main response to critics who demand arguments supporting religious belief has been that no such arguments are needed.

He points out that we all have many beliefs that we can't support by argument. The history of philosophy is littered with failed attempts to show, for example, that other people have minds (inner subjective experiences), although all we see is their bodily behavior. We are inclined to think that we can argue by analogy to other minds: I know that my body is accompanied by an experiencing mind, so it's reasonable to assume that the same is true of people with similar bodies. But it's very implausible to argue from one example (me) to a general conclusion about all humans. Similarly, we all believe that material things exist when we aren't experiencing them and that the past is often a reliable guide to the future. As in the case of other minds, we have experiences all the time that lead us to have these beliefs, but no one has yet come up with a compelling argument to show that these experiences establish the beliefs, and are not just comforting illusions. Nonetheless, we all think that we require nothing further to support the beliefs.

Plantinga asks: How does this differ from religious believers who have repeated experiences of what they take to be the reality of God? These experiences are not the spectacular visions and raptures of the mystics, just an everyday sense of God's presence, what John Calvin called a *sensus divinitatis*. Of course, not everyone has this sort of religious experience, and there's no reason for those who don't have the experience to agree with those who do. But, Plantinga maintains, the large number of believers who do have such experiences have every intellectual right to their theist belief.

As to the problem of evil, Plantinga's most important contribution has been a detailed and rigorous effort to respond to *the logical problem of evil*: the claim that believers fall into a logical contradiction when they assert that an all-good, all-powerful God exists while at the same time acknowledging the obvious evils we find in the world. According to the logical problem of evil, it is simply impossible for such a God to exist in a world of evil. As the ancient Greek philosopher Epicurus put it, an all-good God would want to eliminate evil, and an all-powerful God would be able to do so; therefore, if there is such a God, there can be no evil. Since there obviously is evil in the world, God does not exist.

Plantinga deployed a sophisticated knowledge of modal logic (the logic of possibility and impossibility) to develop a complex argument for the logical compatibility of God and evil. Most philosophers have found this argument convincing, but discussion has since moved to *the probabilistic problem of evil*, which claims that, even if it's *possible* for God and evil to coexist, the reality of evil at least makes God's existence highly *improbable*. On this point, which is likely the problem that concerns most ordinary people, there is strong disagreement among philosophers, with arguments that spin into subtle complexities of the mathematical theory of probability.

In our interview, Plantinga touches on his response to the problem of evil and discusses in some detail his defense of belief without argument. He also offers two important critiques of atheism. First, he says, atheists should at least retreat to agnosticism since, even if there is no decisive case for theism, there is likewise none for atheism. This issue will also come up in later interviews.

Plantinga's second objection to atheism is the striking claim that it's logically inconsistent with the evolutionary materialism that atheists often endorse. Many contemporary atheists are materialists, maintaining not only that God doesn't exist but also that there is nothing immaterial—not even, for example, our minds. Atheism alone does not logically imply materialism. An atheist might even believe in an immaterial soul but deny the existence of God because it's inconsistent with the reality of evil. But nowadays atheism—particularly among philosophers—is often part of an overall materialist viewpoint, which excludes anything immaterial and explains all human abilities and functions in terms of evolution by natural selection.

Darwin himself worried that such a viewpoint might undermine trust in our ability to know the truth: "with me the horrid doubt always arises whether the convictions of man's mind, which has been developed from the mind of the lower animals, are of any value or at all trustworthy" (letter to William Graham 3 July 1881, Darwin Correspondence Project [online]). The Christian apologist C. S. Lewis presented an influential version of this doubt in his 1947 book *Miracles*, arguing that beliefs need not be true to help the species survive. We might, for example, avoid eating poison mushrooms only because we think they are sacred.

Plantinga has developed a detailed argument along these lines using the resources of contemporary epistemology and probability theory. He argues that materialism combined with an evolutionary explanation (via natural selection) of how our beliefs arise, casts serious doubt on the truth of anything we might believe—including atheism. In the interview that follows, he gives a sketch of this argument.

INTERVIEW WITH ALVIN PLANTINGA[*]

Gary Gutting: A recent survey by *PhilPapers*, the online philosophy index, says that 62 percent of philosophers are atheists (with another 11 percent "inclined" to the view). Do you think the philosophical literature provides critiques of theism strong enough to warrant their views? Or do you think philosophers' atheism is due to factors other than rational analysis?

Alvin Plantinga: If 62 percent of philosophers are atheists, then the proportion of atheists among philosophers is much greater than (indeed, is nearly twice as great as) the proportion of atheists among academics generally. (I take atheism to be the belief that there is no such person as the God of the theistic religions.) Do philosophers know something here that these other academics don't know? What could it be? Philosophers, as opposed to other academics, are often professionally concerned with the theistic arguments—arguments for the existence of God. My guess is that a considerable

* This interview was originally published as "Is Atheism Irrational?" in *The Stone* (blog), *New York Times*, February 9, 2014.

majority of philosophers, both believers and unbeliev-
ers, reject these arguments as unsound.

Still, that's not nearly sufficient for atheism. In the
British newspaper *The Independent*, the scientist Richard Dawkins was recently asked the following question: "If you died and arrived at the gates of Heaven,
what would you say to God to justify your life-long
atheism?" His response: "I'd quote Bertrand Russell:
'Not enough evidence, God! Not enough evidence!'"
But lack of evidence, if indeed evidence is lacking, is
no grounds for atheism. No one thinks there is good
evidence for the proposition that there are an even
number of stars; but also, no one thinks the right
conclusion to draw is that there are an uneven number of stars. The right conclusion would instead be
agnosticism.

In the same way, the failure of the theistic arguments, if indeed they do fail, might conceivably be good
grounds for agnosticism, but not for atheism. Atheism,
like even-star-ism, would presumably be the sort of
belief you can hold rationally only if you have strong
arguments or evidence.

G.G.: You say atheism requires evidence to support it.
Many atheists deny this, saying that all they need to
do is point out the lack of any good evidence for theism. You compare atheism to the denial that there are
an even number of stars, which obviously would need
evidence. But atheists say (using an example from Bertrand Russell) that you should rather compare atheism

to the denial that there's a teapot in orbit around the sun. Why prefer your comparison to Russell's?

A.P.: Russell's idea, I take it, is that we don't really have any evidence against teapotism, but we don't need any; the absence of evidence is evidence of absence, and is enough to support ateapotism. We don't need any positive evidence against it to be justified in ateapotism; and perhaps the same is true of theism.

I disagree: Clearly we have a great deal of evidence against teapotism. For example, as far as we know, the only way a teapot could have gotten into orbit around the sun would be if some country with sufficiently developed space-shot capabilities had shot this pot into orbit. No country with such capabilities is sufficiently frivolous to waste its resources by trying to send a teapot into orbit. Furthermore, if some country *had* done so, it would have been all over the news; we would certainly have heard about it. But we haven't. And so on. There is plenty of evidence against teapotism. So if, à la Russell, theism is like teapotism, the atheist, to be justified, would (like the ateapotist) have to have powerful evidence against theism.

G.G.: But isn't there also plenty of evidence against theism—above all, the amount of evil in a world allegedly made by an all-good, all-powerful God?

A.P.: The so-called Problem of Evil would presumably be the strongest (and maybe the only) evidence against theism. It does indeed have some strength; it makes sense to think that the probability of theism, given the existence of all the suffering and evil our world contains, is fairly low. But of course there are also arguments *for* theism. Indeed, there are at least a couple of dozen good theistic arguments. So the atheist would have to try to synthesize and balance the probabilities. This isn't at all easy to do, but it's pretty obvious that the result wouldn't anywhere nearly support straight-out atheism as opposed to agnosticism.

G.G.: But when you say "good theistic arguments", you don't mean arguments that are decisive—for example, good enough to convince any rational person who understands them.

A.P.: I should make clear first that I don't think arguments are needed for rational belief in God. In this regard belief in God is like belief in other minds, or belief in the past. Belief in God is grounded in experience, or in the *sensus divinitatis,* John Calvin's term for an inborn inclination to form beliefs about God in a wide variety of circumstances.

Nevertheless I think there are a large number—maybe a couple of dozen—of pretty good theistic arguments. None is conclusive, but each, or at any rate the whole bunch taken together, is about as strong as philosophical arguments ordinarily get.

G.G.: Could you give an example of such an argument?

A.P.: One presently rather popular argument: fine-tuning. Scientists tell us that there are many properties our universe displays such that if they were even slightly different from what they are in fact, life, or at least our kind of life, would not be possible. The universe seems to be fine-tuned for life. For example, if the force of the Big Bang had been different by 1 part in 1060, life of our sort would not have been possible. The same goes for the ratio of the gravitational force to the force driving the expansion of the universe: If it had been even slightly different, our kind of life would not have been possible. In fact, the universe seems to be fine-tuned, not just for life but for intelligent life. This fine-tuning is vastly more likely given theism than given atheism.

G.G.: But even if this fine-tuning argument (or some similar argument) convinces someone that God exists, doesn't it fall far short of what at least Christian theism asserts, namely the existence of an all-perfect God? Since the world isn't perfect, why would we need a perfect being to explain the world or any feature of it?

A.P.: I suppose what you're thinking is that it is suffering and sin that make this world less than perfect. But then your question makes sense only if the best possible worlds contain no sin or suffering. And is that true? Maybe the best worlds contain free creatures, some of whom sometimes do what is wrong. Indeed, maybe the best worlds contain a scenario very like the Christian story.

Think about it: The first being of the universe, perfect in goodness, power, and knowledge, creates free creatures. These free creatures turn their backs on him, rebel against him and get involved in sin and evil. Rather than treat them as some ancient potentate might—for example, having them boiled in oil—God responds by sending his son into the world to suffer and die so that human beings might once more be in a right relationship to God. God himself undergoes the enormous suffering involved in seeing his son mocked, ridiculed, beaten and crucified. And all this for the sake of these sinful creatures.

I'd say a world in which this story is true would be a truly magnificent possible world. It would be so good that no world could be appreciably better. But then the best worlds contain sin and suffering.

G.G.: OK, but in any case, isn't the theist on thin ice in suggesting the need for God as an explanation of the universe? There's always the possibility that we'll find a scientific account that explains what we claimed only God could explain. After all, that's what happened when Darwin developed his theory of evolution. In fact, isn't a major support for atheism the very fact that we no longer need God to explain the world?

A.P.: Some atheists seem to think that a sufficient reason for atheism is the fact (as they say) that we no longer need God to explain natural phenomena—lightning and thunder, for example. We now have science.

As a justification of atheism, this is pretty lame. We no longer need the moon to explain or account for lunacy; it hardly follows that belief in the nonexistence of the moon (amoonism?) is justified. Amoonism on this ground would be sensible only if the sole ground for belief in the existence of the moon was its explanatory power with respect to lunacy. (And even so, the justified attitude would be agnosticism with respect to the moon, not amoonism.) The same thing goes with belief in God: Atheism on this sort of basis would be justified only if the explanatory power of theism were the only reason for belief in God. And even then, agnosticism would be the justified attitude, not atheism.

G.G.: So, what are the further grounds for believing in God, the reasons that make atheism unjustified?

A.P.: The most important ground of belief is probably not philosophical argument but religious experience. Many people of very many different cultures have thought themselves in experiential touch with a being worthy of worship. They believe that there is such a person, but not because of the explanatory prowess of such belief. Or maybe there is something like Calvin's *sensus divinitatis*. Indeed, if theism is true, then very likely there *is* something like the *sensus divinitatis*. So claiming that the only sensible ground for belief in God is the explanatory quality of such belief is substantially equivalent to assuming atheism.

G.G.: If, then, there isn't evidence to support atheism, why do you think so many philosophers—presumably highly rational people—are atheists?

A.P.: I'm not a psychologist, so I don't have any special knowledge here. Still, there are some possible explanations. Thomas Nagel, a terrific philosopher and an unusually perceptive atheist, says he simply doesn't *want* there to be any such person as God. And it isn't hard to see why. For one thing, there would be what some would think was an intolerable invasion of privacy: God would know my every thought long before I thought it. For another, my actions and even my thoughts would be a constant subject of judgment and evaluation.

Basically, these come down to the serious limitation of human autonomy posed by theism. This desire for autonomy can reach very substantial proportions, as with the German philosopher Heidegger, who, according to Richard Rorty, felt guilty for living in a universe he had not himself created. Now, there's a tender conscience! But even a less monumental desire for autonomy can perhaps also motivate atheism.

G.G.: Especially among today's atheists, materialism seems to be a primary motive. They think there's nothing beyond the material entities open to scientific inquiry, so there's no place for immaterial beings such as God.

A.P.: Well, if there are only material entities, then atheism certainly follows. But there is a really serious problem for materialism: It can't be sensibly believed, at least if, like most materialists, you also believe that humans are the product of evolution.

G.G.: Why is that?

A.P.: I can't give a complete statement of the argument here. But roughly, here's why: First, if materialism is true, human beings, naturally enough, are material objects. Now what, from this point of view, would a *belief* be? My belief that Marcel Proust is more subtle than Louis L'Amour, for example? Presumably this belief would have to be a material structure in my brain—say, a collection of neurons that sends electrical impulses to other such structures as well as to nerves and muscles, and receives electrical impulses from other structures.

But in addition to such neurophysiological properties, this structure, if it is a belief, would also have to have a *content*: It would have, say, to be the belief that *Proust is more subtle than L'Amour.*

G.G.: So is your suggestion that a neurophysiological structure can't be a belief? That a belief has to be somehow immaterial?

A.P.: That may be, but it's not my point here. I'm interested in the fact that beliefs cause (or at least partly cause) actions. For example, my belief that there is a beer in the fridge (together with my desire to have a beer) can cause me to heave myself out of my comfortable armchair and lumber over to the fridge.

But here's the important point: It's by virtue of its material, neurophysiological properties that a belief causes the action. It's in virtue of those electrical signals sent via efferent nerves to the relevant muscles, that the belief about the beer in the fridge causes me to go to the fridge. It is *not* by virtue of the content (*there is a beer in the fridge*) the belief has.

G.G.: Why do you say that?

A.P.: Because if this belief—this structure—had had a totally different content (even, say, if it was a belief that *there is no beer in the fridge*) but had the same neurophysiological properties, it would still have caused that same action of going to the fridge. This means that the content of the belief isn't a cause of the behavior. As far as causing the behavior goes, the content of the belief doesn't matter.

G.G.: That does seem to be a hard conclusion to accept. But won't evolution get the materialist out of this difficulty? For our species to have survived, presumably many, if not most, of our beliefs must be true—otherwise, we wouldn't be functional in a dangerous world.

A.P.: Evolution will have resulted in our having beliefs that are adaptive; that is, beliefs that cause adaptive actions. But as we've seen, if materialism is true, the belief does not cause the adaptive action by way of its content: It causes that action by way of its neurophysiological properties. Hence it doesn't matter what the content of the belief is, and it doesn't matter whether that content is true or false. All that's required is that the belief have the right neurophysiological properties. If it's also true, that's fine; but if false, that's equally fine.

Evolution will select for belief-producing processes that produce beliefs with adaptive neurophysiological properties, but not for belief-producing processes that produce true beliefs. Given materialism and evolution, any particular belief is as likely to be false as true.

G.G.: So your claim is that if materialism is true, evolution doesn't lead to most of our beliefs being true.

A.P.: Right. In fact, given materialism and evolution, it follows that our belief-producing faculties are not reliable.

Here's why: If a belief is as likely to be false as to be true, we'd have to say the probability that any particular belief is true is about 50 percent. Now, suppose we had a total of 100 independent beliefs (of course, we have many more). Remember that the probability that all of a group of beliefs are true is the multiplication of all their individual probabilities. Even if we set a fairly low bar for reliability—say, that at least two-thirds (67 percent) of our beliefs are true—our overall reliability, given materialism and evolution, is exceedingly low: something like .0004. So if you accept both materialism and evolution, you have good reason to believe that your belief-producing faculties are not reliable.

But to believe that is to fall into a total skepticism, which leaves you with no reason to accept any of your beliefs (including your beliefs in materialism and evolution!). The only sensible course is to give up the claim leading to this conclusion: that both materialism and evolution are true. Maybe you can hold one or the other, but not both.

So if you're an atheist simply because you accept materialism, maintaining your atheism means you have to give up your belief that evolution is true. Another way to put it: The belief that both materialism and evolution are true is self-refuting. It shoots itself in the foot. Therefore it can't rationally be held.

FURTHER THOUGHTS

Divine sensibility

Although many philosophically reflective believers have endorsed Plantinga's account of a divine sensibility, others have rejected it, often arguing that the approach would require accepting as rational all sorts of crazy beliefs, even those like the belief of Linus (Charlie Brown's friend in the *Peanuts* cartoons) in a Great Pumpkin that brings children candy on Halloween. Others note that, even if religious experiences support belief in a "basic God" (e.g., a good and powerful being who cares about us), they can't support anything like detailed theological claims about God's nature or his miraculous intervention in the world. Subsequent interviews with Louise Antony and Keith DeRose will further discuss this issue.

Atheism or agnosticism?

Plantinga's case against atheism argues first that, assuming a lack of evidence either for or against God's existence, agnosticism is a more rational position than atheism. In assessing this argument, an important question is whether atheists claim to *know* that God does not exist. Atheists often insist that they don't claim to know that there is no God, just that God's existence is highly improbable. Sometimes their point is that knowledge requires complete (100 percent) certainty, sometimes that "it isn't possible to prove a negative".

There are some contexts in which we do use "know" to express total certainty: "Although the odds are ten million to one against my winning the lottery, I still don't know that I won't win" (if I did, why would I buy a ticket?). But in most contexts, we can claim to know what is only highly justified (very probable): "I know that I'm not going to win this year's Nobel Prize for physics". More broadly, requiring 100 percent certainty would mean that there's no such thing as scientific knowledge.

As to the impossibility of proving a negative, notice that the statement "You can't prove a negative" is itself a negative; so if it's true, there's no way of proving it. But that's a problem only if "proof" requires 100 percent certainty. In most cases, as we've seen, a proof (yielding knowledge) need only show a high probability. In this sense, we can prove that many existence claims are false. For example, we know that there are no McDonald's beyond the Earth, and that no human being has ever lived for a thousand years.

The question, then, is whether atheists have good reason for denying the existence of God, even if they can't be absolutely certain. The "New Atheists" (for example, Richard Dawkins, Christopher Hitchens, and Sam Harris) have popularized the view that the only "evidence" required to establish atheism is the *lack of evidence for theism*. In our interview, Plantinga argues against this claim, but the issue needs further discussion and is taken up in later interviews.

2

A CASE FOR ATHEISM

(LOUISE ANTONY)

Louise Antony is especially prominent for her work in philosophy of mind, epistemology, and feminist philosophy. She also edited *Philosophers Without Gods* (Oxford University Press, 2007), a collection of essays by atheists who are professional philosophers. The first part of the book offers personal reflections on how and why the authors became atheists, the second part less personal critiques of religious belief. Antony's own essay engagingly describes how her first philosophy course undermined the Catholic faith in which she had been raised. She was deeply troubled by the problem of evil, and finally gave up belief when she encountered persuasive arguments that morality didn't require belief in God.

Our interview primarily centers on the question of disagreement about religious claims. Disagreement has recently become a lively area of philosophical discussion in the theory of knowledge (epistemology). The focus has been disagreement between what philosophers call "epistemic peers": those who seem equally competent to judge a disputed question but have arrived at conflicting conclusions. As Jennifer Lackey puts it, epistemic peers "are equally familiar with the evidence and arguments that bear on [a given] question, and they are equally competent, intelligent, and fair-minded in their assessment of the evidence and arguments that are relevant to this question" ("Disagreement and Belief Dependence," in David Christensen and Jennifer Lackey, eds., *The Epistemology of Disagreement: New Essays*, Oxford University Press, 2013). Such disagreements are common both in personal life ("Should we risk inviting the Joneses to our dinner party?", "Did I really promise to paint the house this summer?") and in public debates ("Are current economic inequalities unjust?", "Does climate change constitute an international crisis?"). A couple may disagree on the personal issues, just as distinguished experts may disagree on the public issues, with there being no apparent reason to prefer the views of either side. Religion, of course, is a prime example of disagreement among peers, with highly informed and acute philosophers on both sides of the issue.

In our interview, Antony suggests a way of avoiding the problem of disagreement. The idea that I have epistemic peers is an abstraction, an idealization that is never realized: "The whole notion of 'epistemic peers' belongs only to the abstract study of knowledge, and has no role to play in real life." Quibblers may argue that there surely are simple cases (like the restaurant check discussed in "Further Thoughts" below) where, for the practical purpose at hand, there are epistemic peers. But isn't it at least plausible that in complex and fundamental disagreements on major issues—like religion—there are no epistemic peers? Who could equal me as a judge of what beliefs are supported by my own distinctive perspective and experiences? Of course, I need to beware of self-deception, but a judgment about such a personally vital issue nonetheless seems to require the interior, subjective viewpoint that only I can have.

This move from objectivity to subjectivity raises perhaps the most difficult but also most important issue about belief in God. Is religion at root about what exists "out there" in the world, or is it about the truth I find within me? Some of the greatest religious thinkers have insisted that this truth is "interior" (Augustine) or "subjective" (Kierkegaard). But doesn't this "subjective turn" reduce religion to a kind of moral psychology, stripping away its strong metaphysical claims about a transcendent God who literally created the world and intervenes in its history? This issue emerges at the end of the interview when Antony questions whether it makes any real difference whether we believe in God or not. Why, she asks, should disagreement about what sorts of things exist have any "moral significance"— any effect on how we should live? This apparent split between meaning and metaphysics, between God as moral inspiration and God as maker of the world, will become central in the interviews that follow with John Caputo and Howard Wettstein.

INTERVIEW WITH LOUISE ANTONY[*]

Gary Gutting: You've taken a strong stand as an atheist, so you obviously don't think there are any good reasons to believe in God. But I imagine there are philosophers

* This interview was originally published as "Arguments Against God" in *The Stone* (blog), *New York Times*, February 25, 2014.

whose rational abilities you respect who are theists. How do you explain their disagreement with you? Are they just not thinking clearly on this topic?

Louise Antony: I'm not sure what you mean by saying that I've taken a "strong stand as an atheist". I don't consider myself an agnostic; I claim to know that God doesn't exist, if that's what you mean.

G.G.: That is what I mean.

L.A.: OK. So the question is, why do I say that theism is *false*, rather than just unproven? Because the question has been settled to my satisfaction. I say "There is no God" with the same confidence I say "There are no ghosts" or "There is no magic." The main issue is supernaturalism—I deny that there are beings or phenomena outside the scope of natural law.

That's not to say that I think everything is within the scope of *human knowledge*. Surely there are things not dreamt of in our philosophy, not to mention in our science—but *that* fact is not a reason to believe in supernatural beings. I think many arguments for the existence of a God depend on the insufficiencies of human cognition. I readily grant that we have cognitive limitations. But when we bump up against them, when we find we cannot explain something—like why the fundamental physical parameters happen to have the values that they have—the right conclusion to draw is that we just can't explain the thing. That's the proper place for agnosticism and humility.

But getting back to your question: I'm puzzled why you are puzzled how rational people could disagree about the existence of God. Why not ask about disagreements among theists? Jews and Muslims disagree with Christians about the divinity of Jesus; Protestants disagree with Catholics about the virginity of Mary; Protestants disagree with Protestants about predestination, infant baptism, and the inerrancy of the Bible. Hindus think there are many gods, while Unitarians think there is at most one. Don't all these disagreements demand explanation too? Must a Christian Scientist say that Episcopalians are just not thinking clearly? Are you going to ask a Catholic if she thinks there are no good reasons for believing in the angel Moroni?

G.G.: Yes, I do think it's relevant to ask believers why they prefer their particular brand of theism to other brands. It seems to me that, at some point of specificity, most people don't have reasons beyond being comfortable with one community rather than another. I think it's at least sometimes important for believers to have a sense of what that point is. But people with many different specific beliefs share a belief in God—a supreme being who made and rules the world. You've taken a strong stand against that fundamental view, which is why I'm asking you about that.

L.A.: Well I'm challenging the idea that there's one fundamental view here. Even if I could be convinced that supernatural beings exist, there'd be a whole separate issue about how many such beings there are and what those beings are like. Many theists think they're home free with something like the argument from design: that there is empirical evidence of a purposeful design in nature. But it's one thing to argue that the universe must be the product of some kind of intelligent agent; it's quite something else to argue that this designer was all-knowing and omnipotent. Why is that a better hypothesis than that the designer was pretty smart but made a few mistakes? Maybe (I'm just cribbing from Hume here) there was a committee of intelligent creators who didn't quite agree on everything. Maybe the creator was a student god, and only got a B minus on this project.

In any case though, I don't see that claiming to know that there is no God requires me to say that no one could have good reasons to believe in God. I don't think there's some general answer to the question "Why do theists believe in God?" I expect that the explanation for theists' beliefs varies from theist to theist. So I'd have to take things on a case-by-case basis.

I have talked about this with some of my theist friends, and I've read some personal accounts by theists, and in those cases, I feel that I have some idea why they believe what they believe. But I can allow there are arguments for theism that I haven't considered, or objections to my own position that I don't know about. I don't think that when two people take opposing stands on any issue that one of them *has* to be irrational or ignorant.

G.G.: No, they may both be rational. But suppose you and your theist friend are equally adept at reasoning, equally informed about relevant evidence, equally honest and fair-minded—suppose, that is, you are what philosophers call epistemic peers: equally reliable as knowers. Then shouldn't each of you recognize that you're no more likely to be right than your peer is, and so both retreat to an agnostic position?

L.A.: Yes, this is an interesting puzzle in the abstract: How could two epistemic peers—two equally rational, equally well informed thinkers—fail to converge on the same opinions? But it is not a problem in the real world. In the real world, there are no epistemic peers—no matter how similar our experiences and our psychological capacities, no two of us are exactly alike, and *any* difference in either of these respects can be rationally relevant to what we believe.

G.G.: So is your point that we always have reason to think that people who disagree are not epistemic peers?

L.A.: It's worse than that. The whole notion of "epistemic peers" belongs only to the abstract study of knowledge, and has no role to play in real life. Take the notion of "equal cognitive powers": speaking in terms of real human minds, we have no idea how to seriously compare the cognitive powers of two people.

G.G.: OK, on your view we don't have any way to judge the relative reliability of people's judgments about whether God exists. But the question still remains, why are you so certain that God doesn't exist?

L.A.: Knowledge in the real world does not entail either certainty or infallibility. When I claim to know that there is no God, I mean that the question is settled to my satisfaction. I don't have any doubts. I don't say that I'm agnostic, because I disagree with those who say it's not possible to know whether or not God exists. I think it's possible to know. And I think the balance of evidence and argument has a definite tilt.

G.G.: What sort of evidence do you have in mind?

L.A.: I find the "argument from evil" overwhelming—that is, I think the probability that the world we experience was designed by an omnipotent and benevolent being is a zillion times lower than that it is the product of mindless natural laws acting on mindless matter. (There are minds in the universe, but they're all finite and material.)

G.G.: Why do you think other philosophers don't see it that way?

L.A.: To cite just one example, Peter van Inwagen, my friend and former teacher, assesses the situation very differently. He believes that we do not and cannot know the probability that the world we experience was designed by an omnipotent and benevolent being (which I estimate as close to zero), and that therefore the existence of suffering in our world gives us no reason to doubt the existence of God. He and I will be arguing about this in a seminar this coming summer, and I look forward to it. Don't bet on either one of us changing our mind, though.

G.G.: What about positive cases for God's existence? When I interviewed Alvin Plantinga, he cited religious experiences as making a strong case for theism. Mightn't it be that he has evidence on this issue that you don't?

L.A.: Many theists I've talked to—including Plantinga—say that they have or have had experiences in which they have become aware of the presence of God. I've never had such experiences.

G.G.: That doesn't mean that Plantinga and others haven't had such experiences.

L.A.: OK, if you hold my feet to the fire (which is what you're doing), I'll admit that I believe I know what sort of experiences the theists are talking about, that I've had such experiences, but that I don't think they have the content the theists assign to them. I've certainly had experiences I would call "profound." Many were aesthetic in nature—music moves me tremendously, and so does nature. I've been tremendously moved by demonstrations of personal courage (not mine!), generosity, sympathy. I've had profound experiences of solidarity, when I feel I'm really together with other people working for some common goal. These are very exhilarating and inspiring experiences, but they are very clearly about human beings—human beings at their best.

G.G.: Would you say, then, that believers who think they have good reasons for theism are deceiving themselves, that they are actually moved by, say, hopes and fears—emotions—rather than reasons?

L.A.: I realize that some atheists do say things like "theists are just engaged in wishful thinking—they can't accept that death is the end". Theists are insulted by such conjectures (which is all they are) and I don't blame them. It's presumptuous to tell someone else why she believes what she believes—if you want to know, start by *asking her.*

It is disrespectful, moreover, to insist that someone else's belief has some hidden psychological cause, rather than a justifying reason, behind it. As a "lapsed Catholic," I've gotten a fair amount of this sort of thing myself: I've been told—sometimes by people who've just met me or who have never met me at all but found out my email address—that I "only" gave up my faith because (a) the nuns were too strict, (b) I wanted to have sex, or (c) I was too lazy to get up on Sundays to go to church.

I believe I have reasons for my position, and I expect

that theists believe they have reasons for theirs. Let's agree to pay each other the courtesy of attending to the particulars.

G.G.: But when you talk about reasons in this way, you seem to mean something like "personal reasons"— reasons that convince you but that you don't, and shouldn't, expect to convince other people. And you agree that theists can and do have reasons in the same sense that you do. Many atheists hold a much stronger view: that they have good reasons and theists don't. Do you agree with this?

L.A.: No, I don't think reasons are "personal" in the sense you mean. Justificatory relations are objective. But they are complex. So whether any given belief justifies another is something that depends partly on what other beliefs the believer has. Also, there may be— objectively—many different but equally reasonable ways of drawing conclusions on the basis of the same body of evidence.

It's likely that the conscious consideration of reasons plays a relatively small role in our acquiring the beliefs we do. An awful lot of what we believe is the result of automatic unconsciousness processing, involving lots of unarticulated judgments. That's perfectly OK a lot of the time—if the process is reliable, we don't have to be able to articulate reasons. I think the proper place for reasons—for demanding and giving reasons—is in interpersonal interaction.

G.G.: What do you mean by that?

L.A.: Reasons are the answer I give to someone who asks me why I believe something, or—more urgently—to someone who asks why *she* ought to believe something that I've asserted. In the public sphere, I think reasons are extremely important. If I'm advocating a social policy that stems from some belief of mine, I need to be able to provide compelling reasons for it—reasons that I can expect a rational person to be moved by. If I refuse to give my employees insurance coverage for contraception because I think contraception is wrong, then I ought—and this is a *moral* ought—to be able to articulate reasons for this position. I can't just say, "That's my belief, and that's that." A sense of responsibility about one's beliefs, a willingness to defend them if challenged, and a willingness to listen to the reasons given by others is one of the guiding ideals of civil society.

G.G.: But doesn't a belief in God often lead people to advocate social policies? For some people, their beliefs about God lead them to oppose gay marriage or abortion. Others' beliefs lead them to oppose conservative economic policies. On your view, then, aren't they required to provide a rational defense of their religious belief in the public sphere? If so, doesn't it follow that their religious belief shouldn't be viewed as just a personal opinion that's nobody else's business?

L.A.: No one needs to defend their religious beliefs to me—not unless they think that those beliefs are *essential* to the defense of the policy they are advocating. If the only argument for a policy is that Catholic doctrine says it's bad, why should a policy that applies to everyone reflect that particular doctrine? "Religious freedom" means that no one's religion gets to be the boss.

But usually, religious people who become politically active think that there are good moral reasons independent of religious doctrine, reasons that ought to persuade any person of conscience. I think—and many religious people agree with me—that the United States' policy of drone attacks is morally wrong, because it's wrong to kill innocent people for political ends. It's the moral principle, not the existence of God, that they are appealing to.

G.G.: That makes it sounds like you don't think it much matters whether we believe in God or not.

L.A.: Well, I do wonder about that. Why do theists care so much about belief in God? Disagreement over that question is really no more than a difference in philosophical opinion. Specifically, it's just a disagreement about ontology—about what kinds of things exist. Why should a disagreement like that bear any moral significance? Why shouldn't theists just look for allies among us atheists in the battles that matter—the ones concerned with justice, civil rights, peace, etc.—and forget

about our differences with respect to such arcane matters as the origins of the universe?

FURTHER THOUGHTS:
DISAGREEMENT ABOUT RELIGION

The question of disagreement among peers has attracted considerable interest in recent years. Here I provide some background for those interested in pursuing the issue further,
particularly regarding religious belief.

Philosophers often prefer to begin discussions of difficult issues with simple, more tractable examples. Here is an
everyday example put forward by David Christensen that has
become quite important in the academic discussion of epistemic peers:

> You and your friend have been going out to dinner reg-
> ularly for many years. You always tip 20% and split the
> check, and you each do the requisite calculation in
> your head. Most of the time you have agreed, but in the
> instances when you have not, you have taken out a calcu-
> lator to check; over the years, you and your friend have
> been right in these situations equally often. Tonight, you
> figure out that your shares are $43, and become quite con-
> fident of this. But then your friend announces that she is
> quite confident that your shares are $45. Neither of you
> has had more wine or coffee, and you do not feel (nor
> does your friend appear) especially tired or especially
> perky. How confident should you now be that your shares
> are $43? (David Christensen, "Disagreement as Evidence:

The Epistemology of Controversy," *Philosophy Compass* 4/5 [2009], 756–67, p. 757.)

In this simple case, it seems clear that I (and my friend) should withhold judgment about how much we owe until we can agree on a result (that is, by recalculating together or appealing to someone better at math than either of us). This is an example of what is called the *conciliatory* response to disagreement. We admit that neither view is to be preferred and so back away from our own judgments and seek further information or advice.

But, Christensen points out, we may well come to a different conclusion if we tweak our example a bit:

> The situation is as before, but this time you do not do the arithmetic in your head. You do it carefully on paper, and check your results. Then you do it in a different way. Then you take out a well-tested calculator and use it to check the problem a few different ways. Each time you get $43, so you become extremely confident in this answer. But then your friend, who was also writing down numbers and pushing calculator buttons, announces that she has consistently gotten $45! (ibid., 758).

Here it seems reasonable to think: I've done this simple calculation so often and so carefully that for all practical purposes I'm absolutely certain that I haven't made a mistake. Yes, my friend claims to have to have been just as careful, but I know I've been utterly careful and this gives me good reason to think that my friend hasn't been. So I'll stick with my conclusion. This is called the *steadfast* response to disagreement.

These two examples suggest that the proper response when epistemic peers disagree will differ from case to case. So what about the case of belief in God? Should we be conciliatory or steadfast? Here we need to take account of some ways that religious disagreements differ from the simple examples we've been looking at. For one thing, accepting or rejecting a religious belief often has an enormous effect on people. Antony herself says that the day she first heard about the problem of evil "literally changed my life" (*Philosophers Without Gods*, 49). Another point is that there's often little prospect of finding further evidence or arguments that will settle religious questions. Finally, it's highly likely that any religious view I accept will be rejected by a good number of my epistemic peers. From all this, I can conclude that being conciliatory about religious disagreements will almost surely mean that I remain agnostic (permanently withhold judgment) on all religious questions important to me. Many people, both theists and atheists, will find this conclusion unpalatable. Even those who don't will surely balk when they realize that the argument requires agnosticism about not just religion but also all major disputed ethical and political topics.

At this point, we may retort that, at least on major issues like religion, morality, and politics, I should give no weight to what my epistemic peers think. Don't I have a right to my opinion, no matter who might disagree with me? Isn't that what we mean by freedom of thought? True, but the fact that I have a right to think something doesn't mean that it's right to think it. My political or moral right to hold my views doesn't imply that I have good reasons for holding them. Think of it this way: I believe that those I disagree with have a right to their opinions even if I'm sure those opinions are unreasonable.

There's another way to defend steadfastness in disputes about religion and similar fundamental issues. Deep and fundamental convictions—such as religious beliefs—are essential to a person's moral integrity; so it would be shameful for me to renounce my beliefs just because other people don't share them. Pick your favorite moral heroes—say, Socrates, Lincoln, or Gandhi. Does it make sense to say that they should have abandoned their core beliefs when they learned that there were epistemic peers who had contrary convictions? This remains an important question that extends to almost all of our most important beliefs.

3

RELIGION AND DECONSTRUCTION

(JOHN CAPUTO)

Ever since Socrates began quizzing his fellow Athenians, philosophy has been built on intellectual distinctions: different ideas that we need to keep separate in order to think clearly. We all have opinions that we think are right, but an opinion isn't the same as knowledge. Of course we should be free to act, but we shouldn't confuse freedom with the license to do anything. The law tells us what we ought to do, but there's a difference between a civil law and a moral law. The progress of philosophy over the centuries has been largely a matter of discovering and refining the distinctions that allow us to think with clarity and rigor. Even in our first two interviews, we've already seen the importance of distinguishing between atheism and agnosticism, absence of evidence and evidence of absence, subjectivity and objectivity, knowledge and certainty.

But philosophy places no limits on the kinds of questions it might have to ask—recall Socrates's injunction to follow the argument wherever it leads—and philosophers have often been suspicious of distinctions themselves, of the very idea that reality can be caught in the net of our either-or dichotomies. Even before Socrates, Heraclitus insisted on a constant flow that washes away any hard and fast divisions; and especially since Hegel, dialectical thinking has tried to show that even what seem to be the clearest distinctions may turn out to be inadequate (for example, self-contradictory or oversimplified). Such thinking has even led to questioning the very idea that philosophy should seek the sort of clarity and rigor we find in logic and mathematics. In recent years, this distrust of clear distinctions has been especially prominent in the work of the French philosopher Jacques Derrida.

Derrida and those who follow him specialize in *deconstruction*: revealing the tensions, confusions, or contradictions in important concepts. Let's take one of Derrida's most important examples: the concept of a gift. We live much of our lives in a world of economic exchange, with its quid pro quo of buying and selling. A gift, however, is by definition outside the economic circle. A gift is given out of sheer generosity, not for the sake of getting anything in return. I have gained nothing by my gift, and you owe me nothing in return. Of course, there are pseudo-gifts, like the "free gifts" businesses offer us when we buy something else, or when I take you to lunch to soften you up for a favor. But a true gift is free of any such ploys.

Or is it? Derrida argues than even the purest gift, with no ulterior motivation, puts the recipient into my debt. My gift is a gift for you only if you recognize it as such, otherwise it's just a lucky windfall. But your mere recognition of the gift implies your feeling of gratitude; if it didn't, you would perceive it as something else—an offer, an intrusion, maybe even a threat. But gratitude involves a need, even an obligation, to reciprocate: to give a gift in return. At the very instant that a gift is given, the polarity between giver and recipient is reversed. The giver, supposed to be giving without return, is now owed by the recipient, supposed to have received without obligation. We've all received gifts that merely make our hearts fall at the thought of having to reciprocate. But Derrida sees such cases as vivid examples of the underlying logic of any gift. The very structure and possibility of the gift will, he says, "define or produce the annulment, the annihilation, the destruction of the gift." A gift cannot "be what it was except on the condition of not being what it was" (*Given Time: I. Counterfeit Money*, University of Chicago Press, 1994, p. 35).

Derrida himself wrote extensively about religion using his deconstructive approach, and John Caputo has led the way among Anglophone philosophers in interpreting, criticizing, and developing this approach. (See, for example, his *The Prayers and Tears of Jacques Derrida: Religion Without Religion*, Indiana University Press, 1997.) It's easy to conclude that writers like Derrida and Caputo are undermining traditional theistic religion, although Derrida appears uneasily between asserting and denying God (but without withdrawing into agnostic doubt), and Caputo is an avowed, if unorthodox, Catholic.

INTERVIEW WITH JOHN CAPUTO*

Gary Gutting: You approach religion through Jacques Derrida's notion of deconstruction, which involves ques-

---

* This interview was originally published as "Deconstructing God" in *The Stone* (blog), *New York Times*, March 9, 2014.

tioning and undermining the sorts of sharp distinctions traditionally so important for philosophy. What, then, do you think of the distinctions between theism, atheism, and agnosticism?

John Caputo: I would begin with a plea not to force deconstruction into one of these boxes. I consider these competing views as beliefs, creedal positions, that are inside our head by virtue of an accident of birth. There are the people who "believe" things from the religious traditions they've inherited; there are the people who deny them (the atheism you get is pegged to the god under denial); and there are the people who say, "Who could possibly know anything about all of that?" To that I oppose an underlying form of life, not the beliefs inside our head but the desires inside our heart, an underlying faith, a desire beyond desire, a hope against hope, something which these inherited beliefs contain without being able to contain.

If you cease to "believe" in a particular religious creed, like Calvinism or Catholicism, you have changed your mind and adopted a new position, for which you will require new propositions. Imagine a debate in which a theist and an atheist actually convince each other. Then they trade positions and their lives go on. But if you lose "faith," in the sense this word is used in deconstruction, everything is lost. You have lost your faith in life, lost hope in the future, lost heart, and you cannot go on.

G.G.: I'm having some trouble with your use of "deconstruction." On the one hand, it seems to be a matter of undermining sharp distinctions, like that between atheism and theism. On the other hand, your own analysis seems to introduce a sharp distinction between beliefs and forms of life—even though beliefs are surely part of religious ways of life.

J.C.: After making a distinction in deconstruction, the first thing to do is to deconstruct it, to show that it leaks, that its terms are porous and intersecting, one side bleeding into the other, these leaks being the most interesting thing of all about the distinction. I am distinguishing particular beliefs from an underlying faith and hope in life itself, which takes different forms in different places and traditions, by which the particular traditions are both inhabited and disturbed.

I agree they are both forms of life, but on different levels or strata. The particular beliefs are more local, more stabilized, more codified, while this underlying faith and hope in life is more restless, open-ended, disturbing, inchoate, unpredictable, destabilizing, less confinable.

G.G.: OK, I guess you might say that all thinking involves making distinctions, but deconstructive thinking always turns on itself, using further distinctions to show how any given distinction is misleading. But using this sort of language leads to paradoxical claims as, for example, when you say, as you just did, that beliefs con tain a faith that they can't contain. Paradox is fine as long as we have some way of understanding that it's not an outright contradiction. So why isn't it a contradiction to say that there's a faith that beliefs both contain and can't contain?

J.C.: The traditions contain (in the sense of "possess") these events, but they cannot contain (in the sense of "confine" or "limit") them, hold them captive by building a wall of doctrine, administrative rule, orthodoxy, propositional rectitude around them.

G.G.: So the distinction that saves you from contradiction is this: Beliefs contain faith in the sense that, in the world, beliefs are where we find faith concretely expressed; but any given faith can be expressed by quite different beliefs in quite different historical contexts. In this sense, the faith is not contained by the beliefs. That makes sense.

Presumably, then, deconstructive theology is the effort to isolate this "common core" of faith that's found in different historical periods—or maybe even the differing beliefs of different contemporary churches.

J.C.: No! I am not resurrecting the old comparative-religion thesis that there is an underlying transcendental form or essence or universal that we can cull from differing empirical religious beliefs, that can be approached only asymptotically by empirical cases. I am saying that the inherited religious traditions contain something deeper, which is why they are important. I don't marginalize religious traditions; they are our indispensable inheritance. Without them, human experience would be impoverished, its horizon narrowed. We would be deprived of their resources, not know the name of Moses, Jesus, Muhammad, the startling notion of the "kingdom of God," the idea of the messianic and so on.

As a philosopher I am, of course, interested in what happens, but always in terms of what is going on *in* what happens. The particular religious traditions are what happen, and they are precious, but my interest lies in what is going on *in* these traditions, *in* our memory of Jesus, say. But different traditions contain different desires, promises, memories, dreams, futures, a different sense of time and space. Nothing says that underneath they are all the same.

G.G.: That doesn't seem to me what typically goes on in deconstructive theology. The deconstructive analysis of any religious concept—the Christian Trinity, the Muslim oneness of God, Buddhist nirvana—always turns out to be the same: an endless play of mutually undermining differences.

J.C.: There is no such thing as deconstructive theology, in the singular, or "religion," in the singular. There are only deconstructive versions of concrete religious traditions, inflections, repetitions, rereadings, reinventions, which open them up to a future for which they are not prepared, to dangerous memories of a past they try not to recall, since their tendency is to consolidate and to stabilize. Accordingly, you would always be able to detect the genealogy, reconstruct the line of descent, figure out the pedigree of a deconstructive theology. It would always bear the mark of the tradition it inflects.

A lot of the "Derrida and theology" work, for example, has been following the wrong scent, looking for links between Derrida's ideas and Christian negative theology, while missing his irregular and heretical messianic Judaism. I like to joke that Derrida is a slightly atheistic quasi-Jewish Augustinian, but I am also serious.

G.G.: I can see that there are influences of Judaism, Augustinian Christianity, and enlightenment atheism in Derrida. But isn't this just a matter of his detaching certain religious ideas from their theistic core? He talks of a messiah—but one that never comes; he's interested in the idea of confessing your sins—but there's no one to forgive them. After all the deconstructive talk, the law of noncontradiction still holds: Derrida is either an atheist or he isn't. It seems that the only reasonable answer is that he's an atheist.

J.C.: In the middle of his book on Augustine, Derrida said he "rightly passes for an atheist", shying away from a more definitive "I am an atheist". By the standards of the local rabbi, that's correct, that's the position to attribute to him, that's a correct proposition. But if we stop there we miss everything interesting and important about what he is saying for religion and for understanding deconstruction.

G.G.: So if I insist on expressing religious faith in propositions (assertions that are either true or false), then, yes, Derrida's an atheist. But according to you, the propositions that express faith aren't what's interesting or important about religion.

I agree that there's much more to religion than what's stated in creeds. There are rituals, ascetic practices, moral codes, poetry, and symbols. But for most people, believing that God exists entails believing such propositions as that there's someone who guarantees that justice will eventually prevail, that no suffering is without meaning, that there is a life after death where we can find eternal happiness.

J.C.: We have to appreciate the deep distrust that Derrida has for this word "atheism". This kind of normalizing category has only a preliminary value—it finds a place to put him in a taxonomy of "positions"—but it obscures everything that is valuable here. This word is too powerful for him, too violent. That is why in another place he said calling him an atheist is "absolutely ridiculous". His "atheism" is not unlike that of Paul Tillich, when Tillich said that to the assertion that God is a Supreme Being the proper *theological* response is atheism, but that is the beginning of theology for Tillich, not the end.

Derrida is not launching a secularist attack on reli-

gion. Deconstruction has nothing to do with the violence of the "New Atheists" like Richard Dawkins and
Christopher Hitchens. Derrida approaches the mystics,
the scriptures, Augustine with respect—they are always
ahead of him, he says—and he always has something to
learn from them. He is not trying to knock down one
position ("theism") with the opposing position ("atheism"). He does not participate in these wars.

G.G.: You keep saying what Derrida doesn't do. Is there
any positive content to his view of religion or is it all
just "negative theology"? Is he in any sense "making
a case" for religion? Can reading Derrida lead to religious belief?

J.C.: In its most condensed formulation, deconstruction is affirmation, a "yes, yes, come" to the future and
also to the past, since the authentic past is also ahead
of us. It leads to, it is led by, a "yes" to the transforming
surprise, to the promise of what is to come in whatever
we have inherited—in politics, art, science, law, reason
and so on. The bottom line is "yes, come."

Derrida is reading, rereading, reinventing inherited
texts and traditions, releasing the future they "harbor",
which means both to keep safe but also conceal, all in
the name of what Augustine calls "doing the truth". He
is interested in *all* the things found in the scriptures
and revelation, the narratives, the images, the angels—
not in order to mine them for their "rational content",
to distill them into proofs and propositions, but to allow

them to be heard and reopened by philosophy. Deconstruction is a way to read something meticulously, feeling about for its tensions, releasing what it itself may not want to disclose, remembering something it may not want to recall—it is not a drive-by shooting.

G.G.: But why call this "religion"?

J.C.: Derrida calls this a "religion *without* religion". Other people speak of the "postsecular", or of a theology "after the death of God", which requires first passing through this death. In Derrida's delicate logic of "without", a trope also found in the mystics, a thing is crossed out without becoming illegible; we can still see it through the cross marks. So this religion comes without the religion you just described—it is not nearly as safe, reassuring, heartwarming, triumphant over death, sure about justice, so absolutely fabulous at soothing hearts, as Jacques Lacan says, with an explanation for everything. His religion is risky business, no guarantees.

G.G.: If Derrida doubts or denies that there's someone who guarantees such things, isn't it only honest to say that he is an agnostic or an atheist? For most people, God is precisely the one who guarantees that the things we most fear won't happen. You've mentioned Derrida's interest in Augustine. Wouldn't Augustine—and virtually all the Christian tradition—denounce any suggestion that God's promises might not be utterly reliable?

J.C.: Maybe it disturbs what "most people" think religion is—assuming they are thinking about it—but maybe a lot of these people wake up in the middle of the night feeling the same disturbance, disturbed by a more religionless religion going on *in* the religion meant to give them comfort. Even for people who are content with the contents of the traditions they inherit, deconstruction is a life-giving force, forcing them to reinvent what has been inherited and to give it a future. But religion for Derrida is not a way to link up with saving supernatural powers; it is a mode of being-in-the-world, of being faithful to the promise of the world.

The comparison with Augustine is telling. Unlike Augustine, he does not think a thing has to last forever to be worthy of our unconditional love. Still, he says he has been asking himself all his life Augustine's question, "What do I love when I love my God?" But where Augustine thinks that there is a supernaturally revealed answer to this question, Derrida does not. He describes himself as a man of prayer, but where Augustine thinks he knows to whom he is praying, Derrida does not. When I asked him this question once he responded, "If I knew that, I would know everything"—he would be omniscient, God!

This not-knowing does not defeat his religion or his prayer. It is constitutive of them, constituting a faith that cannot be kept safe from doubt, a hope that cannot be kept safe from despair. We live in the distance between these pairs.

G.G.: But if deconstruction leads us to give up Augustine's way of thinking about God and even his belief in revealed truth, shouldn't we admit that it has seriously watered down the content of Christianity, reduced the distance between it and agnosticism or atheism? Faith that is not confident and hope that is not sure are not what the martyrs died for.

J.C.: In this view, what martyrs die for is an underlying faith, which is why, by an accident of birth or a conversion, they could have been martyrs for the other side. Mother Teresa expressed some doubts about her beliefs, but not about an underlying faith in her work. Deconstruction is a plea to rethink what we mean by religion and to locate a more unnerving religion going on *in* our more comforting religion.

Deconstruction is faith and hope. In what? In the promises that are harbored in inherited names like "justice" and "democracy"—or "God". Human history is full of such names and they all have their martyrs. That is why the difference between Derrida and Augustine cannot be squashed into the distinction between "theism" and "atheism" or—deciding to call it a draw—"agnosticism". It operates on a fundamentally different level. Deconstruction dares to think "religion" in a new way, in what Derrida calls a "new Enlightenment", daring to rethink what the Enlightenment boxed off as "faith" and "reason".

But deconstruction is not destruction. After all, the bottom line of deconstruction, "yes, come", is pretty much the last line of the New Testament: "Amen. Come, Lord Jesus".

FURTHER THOUGHTS:
NEGATIVE THEOLOGY AND DECONSTRUCTION

Caputo briefly mentions a Christian tradition of "negative theology", which in many ways parallels deconstruction. Some further reflection on this tradition will deepen our understanding of the deconstructive approach to belief. Negative theology maintains that every positive assertion about God (e.g., that God is good, has knowledge, or even exists) must be balanced by a negative assertion that God's goodness, knowledge, and existence are infinitely distant from anything we understand by those terms. This is hardly a marginal view, since it's articulated by early Church fathers such as Gregory of Nyssa and, especially, by Thomas Aquinas.

Aquinas, like many proponents of negative theology, insists that there is a third stage of talk about God. For example, after we have both asserted and denied that God is good, we can affirm that God is good "eminently". This means that God is good in a sense that goes beyond our conception of goodness. This is the point at which Derrida and Caputo separate themselves from negative theology. The reason is that negative theology, Derrida says, "is always occupied with letting a supraessential reality go beyond the finite categories of essence and existence, that is, of presence, and always hastens to remind us that, if we deny the predicate of existence to God, it is in order to recognize him as a superior, inconceivable, and ineffable mode of being" (*Speech and Phenomena and*

Other Essays, Northwestern University Press, 1973, 134). Derrida and Caputo regard this jump to the "inconceivable" and "ineffable" as covers for an unwarranted return to theological certainty, now presented as a nonconceptual experience of a reality that is a mystery beyond conceptual understanding. They agree that God must remain irreducibly mysterious, but they contend that this requires us to acknowledge that saying anything of God is a precarious leap allowing no comfort of certainty.

But there is more to religions than theological concepts. As Caputo emphasizes, they are all historically rooted in distinctive historical traditions, which involve narratives (stories of how the tradition originated and developed), practices (private devotions and public rituals), institutions (schools and churches), and positions of authority (elders or priests). The fundamental concepts of a religion are used to formulate doctrines that provide the intellectual accounts needed to justify and explain the practices. As a result, the doctrines are primarily vehicles for sustaining the practices, institutions, and, especially, the system of authority.

But according to Caputo, beyond religious concepts and traditions are what he calls "forms of life", a term that Wittgenstein used occasionally and that other philosophers have adopted in diverse ways. Caputo uses "forms of life" to denote faith in its most concrete expression, what we might call *lived faith*: "not the beliefs inside our head but the desires inside our heart", a faith that, if lost, shipwrecks a life.

A tradition and the beliefs that stabilize and transmit it provide the framework for lived faith. But in contrast to the framework's clarity, stability, and assurance, lived faith is ambiguous, fluid, and questioning. Whereas theological dogmas are the intellectual component of a tradition, the intellectual component of living faith is deconstruction.

We may think of Saint Augustine, a key figure for both Derrida and Caputo, as an exemplar of both aspects of religion. Particularly in his *Confessions*, we see a tension between the struggling individual—aching, exulting, questioning—and the bishop, precisely formulating dogma and authoritatively endorsing it. The bishop may be an essential institutional functionary, but the struggling individual is the man of living faith.

We may object that this dual-aspect view violates the defining deconstructionist intention of undermining all binary distinctions. Caputo and Derrida can, however, reply that this undermining is just another episode in the always self-questioning life of faith. The deeper problem is that what they present as a life of faith is precisely what their tradition—including Augustine himself and many other exemplars of faith—views as a destruction of faith by doubt. For what faith provides is precisely the certainty that God offers us salvation. If we lose salvation, it will be because we have freely rejected it. If we fully trust in God, we can be certain of it. If we doubt, we do not trust God and so do not have faith. This, I suspect, is the way contemporary atheists and agnostics would see the matter. After all, isn't it their doubt (or denial) that distinguishes them from believers?

But perhaps both traditional believers and nonbelievers have misunderstood the meaning of faith. Perhaps, as a good deconstructionist would put it, they both are trapped by what they see as the essential distinction between faith and doubt.

Perhaps, in other words, the believers are much further from faith and the nonbelievers much closer to it than they think. That, no doubt, is the final paradox that Caputo's deconstructionist religion leaves us.

But another reading of deconstruction is that it is just a fancy way of rejecting Christianity and other monotheistic traditions as most believers and nonbelievers have understood them. Of course, a critic may say, deconstructionists like Caputo can extract the supernatural existence claims (God, Jesus's resurrection, heaven, immortality) from Christianity and still maintain its doctrinal formulas and spiritual practices. But the residue would be a shell that contains none of the substance that makes the religion, as Alexander Kinglake put it, "important if true". The shell may enhance our natural life on Earth, but it promises nothing beyond. The sublime drama of salvation ends in anticlimax. On this view, the religion of deconstruction—like many similar naturalistic reductions—seems like the ultimate bait and switch.

4

EXPERIENCE AND BELIEF

(HOWARD WETTSTEIN)

Howard Wettstein and John Caputo start from very different points in both religion and philosophy. Wettstein is Jewish and an analytic philosopher, whereas Caputo is Catholic and works in continental philosophy. As a result they formulate their religious ideas quite differently, but their basic approaches are surprisingly similar. Both have little interest in the standard debates in philosophy of religion about proofs and evidence, and both emphasize instead religion as experience and practice.

Wettstein is concerned with the experience of God rather than the existence of God. We might wonder about the distinction: if I experience a tree, doesn't that mean that there is a tree I'm experiencing, that the tree exists? Of course, here the experience is a matter of sense perception—seeing, touching. But, Wettstein points out, there are other sorts of encounters (experiences, in a sense): A mathematician is constantly involved with numbers, thinking about them, proving theorems about them, perhaps at times more intimately involved with numbers than with the physical world. The mathematician doesn't think that numbers exist in the sense that trees do; you can't bump into them or swing from their branches. The mathematician may in fact have no coherent idea of any sense in which numbers exist. So philosophical debates about the existence of numbers go on, as they have since Plato and Aristotle argued about the question. But mathematicians know that they "live in a world with numbers". Similarly, religious people "live in a world with God" and don't need to worry about philosophical questions about in what sense, if any, we ought to say that God exists.

How much does the analogy with numbers help? Theistic religions such as Judaism think of God as a person; indeed, a person we can talk to (in prayer) and who has spoken to at least some of us (as reported in the scriptures). Wettstein mentions Martin Buber, who made an influential distinction between an "I-it" relation and an "I-thou" relation. An "it" is encountered merely as a thing with which I interact causally, the way two billiard balls collide—a purely external relation, not affecting my subjective core. By contrast, an encounter with a "thou" is intersubjective, creating a shared world with two poles of meaning and value. Such encounters, Buber maintained, were personally transformative, but in ways that we cannot describe in literal conceptual terms.

Most encounters between humans are I-it. We share factual information, give orders, express approval or disapproval. But there are also I-thou encounters—with close friends, lovers, perhaps therapists or gurus—that come to have a special, even if not fully expressible, effect on our lives. We might take such encounters as human models for understanding what believers like Wettstein are talking about when they recount their incomparably deeper experiences of God. The question then becomes whether we can make sense of such encounters without claiming that God exists. This is a major topic in my discussion with Wettstein.

At the same time, Wettstein's approach to religion is at odds with the literal, anthropomorphic understanding of God as a "superized" version of a human being. Thinking of God this way is problematic, first because it conflicts with the religious insistence that God is a mystery beyond our understanding (as Wettstein puts it, in encountering God "I'm over my head"). Further, the anthropomorphic conception makes it hard to avoid atheists' demands for empirical evidence of God's existence, as we would demand evidence for someone who claimed that good and powerful extraterrestrials have guided human history. But Wettstein admits that, for all the problems it raises, the anthropomorphic view of God is "at the heart of religious life".

For Wettstein, this issue comes up particularly regarding the relation of religion to philosophical naturalism. Naturalism is the view that there's nothing beyond the physical entities that can be discovered and explained through empirical science. People who believe in God generally seem to think of God as a spiritual being, existing in a nonphysical domain that is beyond the scope of science. Wettstein, however, insists that such a domain makes no sense to him. "To see God as existing in such a domain is to speak as if he had substance, just not a natural or physical substance. As if he were composed of the stuff of spirit, as are, perhaps human souls. Such talk is unintelligible to me. I don't get it." New Atheists like Richard Dawkins and Daniel Dennett might say the same thing—and think that their atheism is a logical consequence. But Wettstein, as we shall see, argues that they are radically misunderstanding religion.

INTERVIEW WITH HOWARD WETTSTEIN[*]

Gary Gutting: You say you're a naturalist and deny that there are any supernatural beings, yet you're a practicing Jew and deny that you're an atheist. What's going on here? What's a God that's not a supernatural being?

Howard Wettstein: Let's begin with a distinction between participation in a practice and the activity of theorizing, philosophically and otherwise, about the practice. Even an advanced and creative mathematician need not have views about, say, the metaphysical status of numbers. Richard Feynman, the great physicist, is rumored to have said that he lived among the numbers, that he was intimate with them. However, he had no views about their metaphysical status; he was highly skeptical about philosophers' inquiries into such things. He had trouble, or so I imagine, understanding what was at stake in the question of whether the concept of existence had application to such abstractions. Feynman had no worries about whether

---

* This interview was originally published as "Is Belief a Jewish Notion?" in *The Stone* (blog), *New York Times*, March 30, 2014.

he was really thinking about numbers. But "existence" was another thing.

It is this distinction between participation and theorizing that seems to me relevant to religious life.

G.G.: How so?

H.W.: I had a close friend in Jerusalem, the late Rabbi Mickey Rosen, whose relation to God was similarly intimate. To watch him pray was to have a glimpse of such intimacy. To pray with him was to taste it; God was almost tangible. As with Feynman, Mickey had no patience with the philosophers' questions. God's reality went without saying. God's existence as a supernatural being was quite another thing. "Belief," he once said to me, "is not a Jewish notion." That was perhaps a touch of hyperbole. The point, I think, was to emphasize that the propositions we assent to are hardly definitive of where we stand. He asked of his congregants only that they sing with him, song being somewhat closer to the soul than assent.

This brings to mind Buber's emphasis on the distinction between speaking *to* God, something that is readily available to all of us, and significant speech/thought *about* God, something that Buber took to be impossible.

G.G.: But you can't in fact speak to someone who doesn't exist—I can't speak to Emma Bovary, although I can pretend to or think I can. Further, why would you even want to pray to someone you didn't believe exists?

On your account, praying to God seems like playacting, not genuine religious commitment.

H.W.: Were I to suggest that God does not exist, that God fails to exist, then what you suggest would have real purchase. My thought is otherwise; it's rather that "existence" is—pro or con—the wrong idea for God.

My relation to God has come to be a pillar of my life, in prayer, in experience of the wonders and the awfulness of our world. And concepts like the supernatural and transcendence have application here. But (speaking in a theoretical mode) I understand such terms as directing attention to the sublime rather than referring to some nonphysical domain. To see God as existing in such a domain is to speak as if he had substance, just not a natural or physical substance. As if he were composed of the stuff of spirit, as are, perhaps, human souls. Such talk is unintelligible to me. I don't get it.

The theism-atheism-agnosticism trio presumes that the real question is whether God exists. I'm suggesting that the real question is otherwise and that I don't see my outlook in terms of that trio.

G.G.: So what is the real question?

H.W.: The real question is one's relation to God, the role God plays in one's life, the character of one's spiritual life.

Let me explain. Religious life, at least as it is for me, does not involve anything like a well-defined, or even something on the way to becoming a well-defined, concept of God, a concept of the kind that a philosopher could live with. What is fundamental is no such thing, but rather the experience of God, for example in prayer or in life's stunning moments. Prayer, when it works, yields an awe-infused sense of having made contact, or almost having done so. Having made contact, that is, concerning the things that matter most, whether the health and well-being of others, or of the community, or even my own; concerning justice and its frequent absence in our world; concerning my gratefulness to, or praise of, God. The experience of sharing commitments with a cosmic senior partner, sharing in the sense both of communicating and literally sharing, "dreaming in league with God", as A. J. Heschel puts it, is both heady and heartening. Even when that partner remains undefined and untheorized.

G.G.: How could you share commitments with someone—a "senior partner", no less—who wasn't a person?

H.W.: I have been speaking as if God were a person, and such is our experience. However, overlaying this is the sense, sometimes only a dim sense, that somehow God is beyond being a person, that we are over our heads in even raising the question. Do you sense a tension, one that, on the face of it, might make theorizing a tad difficult?

G.G.: I see a tension in religious practice itself. In prayer, you say, you have a sense of God as a person but at the same time a sense that God is perhaps not a person. It seems to me that, if God is not a person, then the religious practice of praying to God isn't what most religious people think it is. It may be edifying, therapeutic, or whatever. But it's not, for example, expressing our thoughts to someone who understands and loves us.

H.W.: I wasn't speaking about what God is, nor do I know what he is. (Remember his enigmatic remark in Exodus 3:14, "I am what I am.") I was addressing my experience, with its strange duality: In prayer, we express our deepest selves to God who understands. I pray, and I mean it. But I am "blessed" with an additional sense that, in so supposing, I'm over my head; I don't know what I'm talking about. Both feelings are real and powerful.

These experiences are not theory-driven. The perceptions and understandings of the religious practitioner are more like the outpourings of a poet than they are like theoretical pronouncements. Moments of insight, illumination, and edification do not necessarily respect one another; illuminating one aspect of a phenomenon may occlude others. Poetry, at its most profound, need not observe consistency.

G.G.: This sounds like Whitman: "Do I contradict myself? Very well, then, I contradict myself." Hardly a philosophical response.

H.W.: The philosophy of religion is, of course, another matter. My approach departs from the way the philosophy of religion has been and is still often pursued, largely as a treatment of the putative metaphysics of religion and then the epistemology needed to support such a metaphysics. For me, religious practice is primary; the philosophical project consists in an elucidation of the significance of that practice and of the religious life that embeds the practice.

G.G.: I agree that some questions philosophers of religion ask have purely theoretical significance. But here the question arises out of religious practice itself. Is there a person I'm praying to? How could that not matter to me, precisely as someone engaged in the practice of praying? Compare: I'm on the phone and suddenly get a sense that the responses I'm hearing are from an automated program, not a human being. That's a matter of practical importance. Why is the case of talking to God different?

H.W.: What I've been suggesting about God's personhood is a special case of the problem of anthropomorphism, the way we are drawn into and out of anthropomorphic characterization of God. Such characterization of God is at the heart of religious life. "Taste and see God's goodness" (Psalms 34:8). And there is also a dark side of anthropomorphic depiction: "I form the light, and create darkness: I make peace, and create evil" (Isaiah 45:7). God's goodness, nurture, and the like, but also his anger, his hiddenness, all of these are available to experience.

Yet religious anthropomorphism coexists with a sense that—while hardly universal, even in my religious community—goes deep: in thinking about God, about what he is, about how he works in our world, we are over our heads. "How the hell do I know why there were Nazis?" protests one of Woody Allen's characters, "I don't even know how the can opener works." And such an attitude reflects itself in the anti-anthropomorphist outlook that is an important if controversial stand in religious thought at least since medieval times. Maimonides's attempt, in "Guide for the Perplexed", to explain away biblical anthropomorphism is a Jewish case in point.

G.G.: Well, personal experience can be hard to explicate. But as you've just said, the inclination to think of God in human terms also comes from the Bible, which certainly often talks of God as acting like a person: expressing love or anger, giving commands, making plans. In fact, much of the Hebrew scriptures are a narrative with God as the major protagonist. Doesn't accepting, as I suppose you do, this narrative of how God dealt with his people require thinking of God in human terms? How else can you make sense of God as an agent intervening in human history?

H.W.: For a philosophical anti-anthropomorphist like Maimonides, the Bible "speaks in the language of the folk". Maimonides takes the phrase from the Talmud (but in quite another connection). It is a medieval theological counterpart to Bishop Berkeley's advice that we ought to "think with the learned and speak with the vulgar".

My own view is different. One way to put what I've been saying: The anthropomorphic is one mode of our access to God. I'm not sure that it's the exclusive biblical mode, but it's close to that. As religiously powerful as it is, the anthropomorphized sense of the divine coexists with the humble sense that we are over are heads. This latter feeling can itself be infused with awe. It can have its own religious power.

At the end of your last question, you raise the difficult issue of God's intervention in human affairs. I can't tackle it here. But we should bear in mind that to speak of God as intervening in history, as with characterizing him as creating, planning, willing, and the like, these are all anthropomorphic.

G.G.: Coming back to the personal experiences that seem to be the core of your religious commitment, what's your response to suggestions that such experiences have some sort of entirely human psychological explanation? Doesn't that thought ever seem plausible to you?

H.W.: That one can explain love of our fellows in psychological terms does not suggest that there is something unreal about our fellows or about what we feel for them. The threat to religion is not from the psychological intelligibility of religious experience; it's from that intelligibility in the service of a reductive account.

Freud argued persuasively, I think, for the psychological explicability of the religious impulse, and for the
psychological needs to which the impulse is responsive.
I'm sure something like that is right but, contrary to
Freud's thinking, it doesn't threaten my own outlook or
even the more usual supernaturalism. God's reality or
existence is compatible with the putative needs.

What would it be like for love to be beyond the reach
of psychology? Perhaps there are romantics who find
such a scenario attractive or compelling. Perhaps this is
due to the sense that a naturalistic explanation would
render null and void the mysteries of love, and similarly,
the magic of religious experience. For Einstein, though,
the awe deepened with increased understanding.

G.G.: So then you can't argue for God's reality or existence as the best explanation of religious experience.

H.W.: That's one way to argue for the reality or existence of God, but it's not my way. Such an argument
is subject to refutation by showing that naturalistically
acceptable reasons can explain our experience, either
in Freud's way or some other. And given the propensity
of the universe to disclose itself increasingly to scientific understanding, this argument seems, among other
things, risky.

Nor do people who are blessed with religious experiences, even the intense ones of the mystic, uniformly
suppose that their experiences are only explicable by
reference to the truth of their religious beliefs. Rowan

Williams points out that Teresa of Avila, a medieval saint and mystic whose life was punctuated by ecstatic experiences, never supposed that her uncanny experiences established the truth of religious claims.

G.G.: You seem to be saying that we could have a complete explanation of religious experience, even assuming there's no God. Isn't this just the case that many naturalists make for atheism?

H.W.: I didn't say that we would have a complete explanation in psychological terms. I'm not easy with the idea of a "complete explanation". Say we had a really satisfying psychological account of, for example, what we experience in a moment of intense love. Say further that this was somehow perfectly correlated with a neurophysiological account. Would this be a complete explanation? Would there be no more questions—"why" questions—to ask about the experience? Couldn't we still be puzzled about the role that love plays in the human emotional economy? Wouldn't we want to know what it says about these creatures, their needs, their frustrations, the things that make life worthwhile for them? I'm not sure that we can ever close the book on our multiple explanatory projects.

The subject requires much more than can be said here. It's important to me, however, that my discomfort with the idea of a phenomenon receiving a once-and-for-all finished explanation is not only in the service of defending religion.

One of my complaints about the New Atheists, like Richard Dawkins, is their reductive tendency. I don't see why the psychological (or more generally naturalistic scientific) explicability of a phenomenon should suggest that questions associated with its meaning are put to rest. Indeed, were I a supernaturalist theist, I would feel no need to resist naturalistic explanation.

Earlier naturalistically inclined philosophers like Dewey and Santayana, by contrast with the New Atheists, appreciate the substantial power for good that religion exercises in people's lives. Needless to say, such appreciation is entirely consistent with a deep appreciation for the negative side of the impact of religion: wars, bigotry, narrow-mindedness, and the rest. Such is the way with institutions of such power.

FURTHER THOUGHTS

Experiencing God

Wettstein expresses the uniqueness of experiencing God by saying that when it comes to God, he's "over his head". The modes of expression—the concepts—available to him fail to convey what God is or what experiencing God is like. The philosopher Ronald de Souza once complained that using language we can't understand is like playing tennis without a net: there is no obstacle to saying anything we want. Daniel Dennett, picking up on the simile, suggests that he might say, for example, "God is a ham sandwich wrapped in tin foil". The theologian no doubt will say that's a ridiculous claim, obviously not true of God. But then, Dennett says, he's entitled to respond: "Oh, do you want the net up for my returns, but not for your serves?" The point is that if, as Wettstein says, "I'm over my head; I don't know what I'm talking about", what's to keep Dennett from saying just anything about God? If the net is up to require him to explain how God might be a ham sandwich, then why isn't it up to require the theologian to explain how, for example, an unchanging God could become angry and how an infinitely good God could order atrocities?

Still, it's hard to avoid the suspicion that there are some standards of appropriateness, although everything we say about God may be inadequate. Some expressions—despite their inadequacy—are distinctly better than others for understanding experiences of God. The parables and poetry of the Bible, for example, are far more effective than Dennett's talk of ham sandwiches. But isn't this poetic understanding a matter of what we should do rather than what we should believe? The understanding seems to be like the command, "You must change your life", that ends Rainer Maria Rilke's great poem "Archaic Torso of Apollo": a moral epiphany that is not a logical conclusion from the poem's stunning description of the ancient fragment. After a religious experience, I may have a better idea of what God wants me to do but still no knowledge of who or what God is. But perhaps religion has no need of this sort of knowledge.

Naturalism

Given his naturalism, Wettstein is committed to the possibility that science can explain religious belief. For example, Freud's psychoanalytic explanation of religion draws on our deep psychic needs, while evolutionary explanations consider the adaptive value of religious beliefs and practices. Wettstein objects only when such explanations are *reductive*. In current philosophical discourse, "reduction" has various meanings, with many subtle subdistinctions and complex debates about each form of reductionism. In the most general sense, reductionism is any claim that one domain of reality can be explained by some other domain. For example, some philosophers hold that everything about the nature and behavior of a society can be explained by the individuals who make up the society: there is no sense in which the society exists beyond the existence of these individuals. Others hold that everyday physical objects (trees, rocks, water) can be explained by the molecules that make them up. Similarly, it is often said that the behavior of molecules is explained by the behavior of atoms, and so on down the chain to elementary particles. The most contested forms of reductionism concern human beings. Can, for example, all our psychological features (beliefs, sensations, emotions, values) be explained by the physiology of our brains and nervous systems?

Even if we agree that one level of reality can be explained by another level (trees by molecules, and so on), there remains the question of whether we can *identify* what is explained with what does the explaining: Are, for example, molecules nothing but collections of atoms? Are our beliefs and values nothing but brain states? In contrast to questions of *explanatory reduction*, these are questions of *metaphysical reduction*.

It's hard to see how any religious views could be consistent with complete explanatory and metaphysical reductions. If, say, elementary particles explain everything that happens and are the only things that exist, there would be no room for people desiring salvation or a God who could save them.

Wettstein goes further in the direction of total reduction than we might think possible for a believer. But he does set two limits to reductive explanations: On the one hand, he doubts that we can ever fully explain anything; and on the other hand, he insists that even a complete explanation of the *existence* of things such as love, freedom, and morality will not account for the *meaning* of these things. Here, the remaining question is whether we can accept a thoroughly naturalist account of existence and still have room for the distinctive sorts of meaning that religions find in human life.

5

Soft Atheism

(philip kitcher)

Philip Kitcher is a major contemporary representative of the pragmatic tradition as developed by William James and John Dewey. His treatment of religion reflects that tradition's open-minded empiricism, insisting that ideas be grounded in experience but recognizing that there are experiences beyond the data of empirical science. He is much more negative toward religion than James, who believed in some sort of divinity, and much closer to Dewey, who was an atheist but endorsed religious language as a way of expressing humanist values. Kitcher is an unequivocal atheist, but presents his view as a "soft atheism", in contrast to the "hard" (militant and unsubtle) atheism of polemicists such as Richard Dawkins, Sam Harris, and Christopher Hitchens. The contrast lies in Kitcher's rejection of what he calls "the claim that religion is noxious rubbish to be buried as deeply, as thoroughly and as quickly as possible" (*Life after Faith: The Case for Secular Humanism*, Yale University Press, 2014, xii). But the softness is merely a matter of more nuance and sensitivity in his critique, which still unequivocally rejects the factual claims of theistic religions. These claims, Kitcher maintains, are demonstrably false and ought to be abandoned. Some religious values are worth preserving, but doctrines about God's existence, nature, and intervention in history are not ultimately necessary to support these values. We should not summarily dispatch religion to the rubbish heap, but we should reduce it to an ethical view that is entirely consonant with what Kitcher calls "a fully secular world".

His core critique deftly combines two often discussed features of religion: the diversity of religious beliefs, and naturalistic ways of explaining them. Debates about belief often center on what we might call mere theism: the claim that the world ultimately depends on a good and powerful being. But theistic religions insist on much more, including central claims that other theistic religions firmly reject. Judaism and Islam say God is strictly one, but Christianity says there are three divine persons; Christianity says that God's revelation culminates with the teachings of Jesus, who was the Messiah foretold by the Jewish prophets; orthodox Judaism says that the Messiah has not yet come, while Islam says that the Koran as revealed to Muhammad is a later and final expression of divine truth; the sacred books of these religions present conflicting ideas about the ritual and moral practices God demands of us. As a result, accepting the core teachings of one religion requires denying at least some core teachings of others.

Such denials would make sense for believers who could make a strong rational case for the specific core beliefs of their religion. If you have a solid case for believing that God is triune, you have good reason to reject the view of Jews and

Muslims. But few believers can make such a case; their commitment is typically a matter of a firm conviction ("faith") produced by their religious training and practice. As Kitcher notes, a firm conviction, based on religious training and practice, is also what believers in other religions have. If, therefore, Christians reject Muslims' beliefs, they must claim that Muslims' education and training did not provide good reasons for believing in Islam, but merely applied social and psychological techniques that produced those beliefs regardless of whether they were true. They offer a naturalistic explanation of their beliefs. But Christians have no answer to Muslims who make the same criticism of Christian beliefs. Kitcher's conclusion is that no theistic religion can consistently support the claim that rival views are false and that its view is true.

INTERVIEW WITH PHILIP KITCHER[*]

Gary Gutting: You have said that you "take religious doctrines to have become incredible". Why do you think that?

Philip Kitcher: An opening clarification: I don't think focusing on religious doctrine, as opposed to religious experience or practice, is always the best way of considering a religious perspective. Nonetheless, most religions do offer doctrines about aspects of the world that go beyond the things of everyday experience. They tell

---

[*] This interview was originally published as "The Case for 'Soft Atheism'" in *The Stone* (blog), *New York Times*, May 15, 2014.

us about gods or spirits or ancestors who return or special forces or sacred qualities of particular places. The most basic reason for doubt about any of these ideas is that (when you understand words in their normal, everyday senses) nobody is prepared to accept *all* of them. Even if you suppose that Judaism, Christianity, and Islam share some common conception of a divine being, the Hindu deities are surely different, the spirits and ancestors of African and Native American religions different again, and that's before we get to Melanesian *mana* or the aboriginal Australian Dreamtime. It's very hard to think that every one of these radically different conceptions picks out some aspect of our cosmos.

So asserting the doctrines of a particular religion, or family of religions, requires denying other contrary doctrines. However, when you consider the historical processes underlying the doctrines contemporary believers accept, those processes turn out to be very similar: Long ago there was some special event, a revelation to remote ancestors. Religious doctrine has been transmitted across the generations, and it's learned by novice believers today. If the devout Christian had been brought up in a completely different environment—among aboriginal Australians or in a Hindu community, say—that person would believe radically different doctrines, and, moreover, come to believe them in a completely parallel fashion. On what basis, then, can you distinguish the profound truth of your doctrines from the misguided ideas of alternative traditions?

G.G.: But as you yourself suggest, doctrines aren't necessarily the most important thing about religions. Many believers see doctrinal pronouncements as just halting ways of expressing experiences of a divine reality—experiences that are largely similar across the varieties of religious doctrines.

P.K.: The trouble with this proposal is that such happenings aren't independent of the religious ideas available in the surrounding culture. Yes, people who grow up in quite different traditions have similar experiences—experiences they take to be religious—but they characterize them using the categories of the religions with which they're familiar. Moreover, as people who have studied religious experience, from William James on, have understood very clearly, an experience someone takes to be an encounter with the divine might have all sorts of psychological causes—and, of course, such experiences are often claimed by people who are psychotic, or who are under the influence of drugs, or who are experiencing severe stress. The point has long been appreciated by the major religions of the world, which have taken pains to distinguish "genuine" experiences from those that might promulgate heresy.

Further, scholars studying the evolution of religious doctrines have learned that important ideas of major religions have been introduced in response to the political requirements of some historical situation—even though Jesus received a Roman punishment (crucifixion), it would not have been a bright idea, in a Rome-dominated world, to pinpoint the Romans as responsible, and the problem was resolved by finding a way to cast blame on the Jews (preparing the way for centuries of prejudice and hostility). Further still, religions today adapt their doctrines so as to recruit particular types of people as converts—proselytizers often target people who have just moved to unfamiliar surroundings and who lack close friends (to cite just one example). The historical route to contemporary religious doctrines is full of transitions that have very little to do with the identification of truth. If you're concerned to believe what is true, you should find all of these doctrines incredible.

G.G.: So you reject all religious doctrines, but you also say that you "resist the claim that religion is noxious rubbish to be buried as deeply, as thoroughly and as quickly as possible". Why is that?

P.K.: The past decade has seen some trenchant attacks on religion, and I agree with many points made by people like Daniel Dennett and Richard Dawkins. (Dennett seems to me clearly the most sophisticated of the New Atheists; much as I admire Dawkins's work in evolutionary biology and in enhancing the public understanding of science, he is more often off-target in his diatribes against religion.) But these atheists have been rightly criticized for treating all religions as if they were collections of doctrines, to be understood in quite literal ways, and for not attending to episodes in which the world's religions have sometimes sustained the unfortunate and campaigned for the downtrodden. The "soft atheism" I defend considers religion more extensively, sympathizes with the idea that secularists can learn from religious practices and recommends sometimes making common cause with religious movements for social justice.

G.G.: So on your view, Dawkins and company don't refute all forms of religion, just unsophisticated literal assertions of religious claims.

P.K.: Yes, I think there's a version of religion, "refined religion," that is untouched by the New Atheists' criticisms, and that even survives my argument that religious doctrines are incredible. Refined religion sees the fundamental religious attitude not as belief in a doctrine but as a commitment to promoting the most enduring values. That commitment is typically embedded in social movements—the faithful come together to engage in rites, to explore ideas and ideals with one another, and to work cooperatively for ameliorating the conditions of human life. The doctrines they affirm and the rituals they practice are justified insofar as they support and deepen and extend the values to which they are committed. But the doctrines are interpreted nonliterally, seen as apt metaphors or parables for informing our understanding of ourselves and our world and for seeing how we might improve both. To say that God made a covenant with Abraham doesn't mean that, long ago, some very impressive figure with a white beard negotiated a bargain with a Mesopotamian pastoralist. It is rather to commit yourself to advancing what is most deeply and ultimately valuable, as the story says Abraham did.

G.G.: And so, since they don't regard them as factual, refined believers don't have to deny the stories and metaphors of other religions.

P.K.: Right, they don't have to pick and choose among the religions of the world. They see all religions as asserting that there is more to the cosmos than is dreamed of either in our mundane thoughts or in our most advanced scientific descriptions. Different cultures gesture toward the "transcendent" facets of reality in their many alternative myths and stories. None of the myths is factually true, although they're all true in the sense that their "fruits for life" are good. Prominent examples of refined believers include William James, Martin Buber, and Paul Tillich, and, in our own day, Karen Armstrong, Robert Bellah, and Charles Taylor. When refined religion is thoroughly embedded, religious tolerance thrives, and often much good work is done.

G.G.: Are you, then, willing to tolerate refined religion as a morally and intellectually respectable position?

P.K.: I see refined religion as a halfway house. In the end, a thoroughly secular perspective, one that doesn't suppose there to be some "higher" aspect of reality to serve as the ground of values (or as the ground of assurance that the important values can be realized), can do everything refined religion can do, without becoming entangled in mysteries and difficult problems. Most important, this positive secular humanism focuses directly on the needs of others, treating people as valuable without supposing that the value derives from some allegedly higher source. The supposed "transcendent" toward which the world's religions gesture is both a distraction and a detour.

To sum up: There is more to religion than accepting as literally true doctrines that are literally false. Humanists think the important achievements of religions at their best—fostering community, articulating and supporting values—should be preserved in fashioning a fully secular world. That secular world ought to emerge from a dialogue between humanism and refined religion, one in which religion isn't thrown on the rubbish heap but quietly metamorphoses into something else.

I'm a humanist first and an atheist second. Because I'm more sympathetic to religion than the prominent New Atheists, I label my position "soft atheism". But perhaps I'm a more insidious foe than Dennett and Dawkins. For instead of ignoring important species of religion, I want to prepare the way for their gradual disappearance.

G.G.: I wonder, though, why you say you're an atheist at all. You find incredible the specific accounts of deity that doctrinal religions assert. But does that mean anything more than that you don't believe any of these accounts? Why take the next, atheistic, step of saying that the accounts are all false? Wouldn't it be more accurate to describe yourself as an agnostic, at least about some doctrinal claims?

P.K.: The clear message of all the conflicting doctrines of the world's religions, when treated nonmetaphorically, is that, even if a "transcendent" should exist, all our categories for describing it are woefully inadequate. To borrow a phrase from the late, great philosopher Bernard Williams, any modestly literal thought about it is "one thought too many". We should therefore reject substantive religious doctrines, one and all, even the minimal ones ("an intelligent source of the world's order", "a creator").

So here's a very simple reason I call myself an "a-theist": theism embodies a very specific way of thinking about the "transcendent," accepted by some but by no means all religious traditions—namely that there's at least one deity—and if you suppose, as I do, that all substantive doctrines about any "transcendent" are wrong, you have to think theism is false.

G.G.: I don't see the logic here. Your premise is "all our categories for describing the transcendent are woefully inadequate", from which you conclude that "all substantive doctrines about any transcendent are wrong". There are all sorts of things that our categories are inadequate for describing, from how bananas taste

to what it means to love someone. We don't conclude
that bananas have no taste or that there's no such thing
as love. In any case, I don't see why you say we should
deny that the transcendent exists rather than taking no
stance on its existence.

P.K.: I don't see the parallel. It seems to me that we
can say quite a lot about love and at least a bit about
bananas. Partly that's because we have plenty of uncon-
troversial experience of both.

But let me try to be more explicit: Why reject the "transcendent" rather than simply taking no stance on the issue
of its reality? I start from the idea that all sorts of human
inquiries, including but not limited to the natural sciences, have given us a picture of the world, and that these
inquiries don't provide evidence for any transcendent
aspect of the universe. Epistemic humility should incline
us to believe that our picture is incomplete, but if someone
proposes that proteins fold into their three-dimensional
configurations with the help of an army of ghostly beings,
I don't think I'm dogmatic in rejecting their suggestion.
So why should I take a different attitude toward the proposal that there's a "transcendent"?

G.G.: One reason is that many people have what they
take to be direct experiences of something that tran-
scends the domain of ordinary and scientific experience.

P.K.: To my mind, the experiences labeled "religious"
come in two main types. There are some best understood

in psychiatric terms. There are others, perhaps the overwhelming majority, that happen to people when they feel a great sense of uplift, often at the rightness of things. After all, experiences of this sort are felt by completely secular people, who classify them without appeal to religious language. As Dewey pointed out, referring such experiences to some special aspect of reality is gratuitous speculation.

G.G.: I have in mind rather experiences people describe as of a transcendent reality—what William James calls experiences of a divine presence. But in addition to religious experience, there are respectable, even if not compelling, philosophical cases for the existence of a transcendent being—e.g., a first cause of the universe, an ultimate source of value, a perfection that must exist.

P.K.: Even if people want to say that they feel a "divine presence" on these occasions, that seems to testify to the pervasive religious ideas that surround them, rather than to any reality beyond the mundane world. As to theistic arguments, some of the world's religions have offered such arguments in support of their doctrines, although often different groups within a religious tradition will differ radically in judgments about the value of these exercises. Rational theology proceeds partly on the basis of principles also used in areas of rigorous inquiry (logical principles, for example) and partly on the basis of metaphysical additions, frequently varying across traditions. To my mind all these metaphysical add-ons are dubious. Indeed, many of them seem purpose-built to generate the desired conclusions. Concepts like that of a "necessary being" are problematic outgrowths of particular parochial traditions. We should think of the arguments of rational theology as supplements to a faith whose sources lie elsewhere (as, I believe, many theologians have always taken them to be).

G.G.: I agree that no theistic arguments are compelling, but I don't agree that they all are logically invalid or have obviously false premises. I think the best arguments (especially, sophisticated versions of the cosmological argument) are dubious only in the sense that they use premises (e.g., any contingent thing requires a cause) that are not obviously true but that a rational person might properly believe. But settling our disagreement on this would require a thorough discussion of particular arguments.

P.K.: I agree that working that through would take a lot of words. But quite apart from that, I think religion at its best—the religion that prompts my admiration and sympathy—detaches itself from dubious metaphysics and from speculations about a "transcendent" to which our concepts are surely inadequate. It focuses on human problems, attempting to relieve want and misery, to provide opportunities for worthwhile life, and to deepen and extend important values. Pragmatist that I am, I have little sympathy for strained discussions about whether God had to allow evil in order to create beings with free will, and even less for cheap gibes to the effect that religious faith is analogous to a child's belief in the Easter Bunny. Let's be inspired by the world's collection of religious metaphors insofar as they help us improve the human situation. Humanism first, atheism second. The atheism I favor is one in which literal talk about "God" or other supposed manifestations of the "transcendent" comes to be seen as a distraction from the important human problems—a form of language that quietly disappears.

FURTHER THOUGHTS

Diversity and mystery

Kitcher's core case against the truth of religions is based, as we have seen, on the contradictions between their doctrines. A common response to this sort of objection is, as we also saw, that there is a core of belief common to all major religions and that only this core is essential. Contradictory doctrinal claims may reflect local customs and attitudes but are not part of the universal truths that provide the path to salvation. This universalism is attractively irenic, but it drains almost all of the doctrinal content from the major Western religions. As we shall see in later interviews, Buddhism is an atheistic religion, offering no god as focus of belief; and Hinduism, despite numerous spiritual beings active in the world, has no room for the sort of Supreme Person that is at the heart of the great monotheistic faiths. Unless our universalism arbitrarily excludes the billions who follow these faiths, we will have to allow that a personal God is not essential to the Jewish, Christian, and Muslim religions. The universalist core will likely turn out to be a basic moral code tied to a vaguely characterized transcendent reality—a notion of religion scarcely removed from agnosticism or atheism, and with little resemblance to the religions most people practice. As Kitcher suggests, once the content of religion is so reduced, we can expect that it will eventually be replaced by a thoroughly secular morality.

A seemingly less pallid response appeals to the mystery and incomprehensibility that religions typically ascribe to their teachings. Pascal, for example, says, "If there is a God, He is infinitely incomprehensible, since, having neither parts nor limits, He has no affinity with us." This view was extensively developed by medieval theologians, especially Thomas Aquinas, who insisted that no literal assertion we make about God is strictly true. It must instead be understood "analogously", applying to God in a "higher" sense we could never adequately grasp.

Given such a view, we can argue that the central teaching of all religions may well be true in the sense that they are helpful but distinctly inadequate adumbrations of the incomprehensible nature of the ultimate reality. Their contradictions of one another merely reflect the inadequacy of any formulation. This fits nicely with the medieval notion of "negative theology" according to which any assertion about God must be balanced by a denial of that assertion. (For more on this, see my "Further Thoughts" following the interview with John Caputo.) But the appeal to incomprehensibility risks undermining the intelligibility of religious teachings. How, for example, can we make sense of the crucial theistic claim that

God's creation is "good" if we don't really understand what that term means when we talk about God? Might it be that what God sees as good would be evil in any understanding that we could have? The appeal to mystery may be the best response to Kitcher's argument from the diversity of beliefs, but everything will depend on the ability of religious thinkers to walk the line between ultimate incomprehensibility and sheer unintelligibility.

In our interview, Kitcher in fact cites this appeal to incomprehensibility to support his atheism: "even if a 'transcendent' should exist, all our categories for describing it are woefully inadequate. . . . We should therefore reject substantive religious doctrines, one and all". In the interview, this leads to the question of whether Kitcher's view is atheistic or just agnostic. Since this issue comes up at other points (for example, my interviews with Maudlin and with Garber), it will be worthwhile to pursue the issue a bit further here.

Atheism or agnosticism?

A theist asserts that God exists, whereas an atheist asserts that God does not exist, and an agnostic takes a neutral position, neither asserting nor denying that God exists. Put this way, it would seem that asserting either theism or atheism gives you a burden of proof: you need to give some reason (evidence or argument) in defense of your assertion. Therefore, if you don't make a good case for atheism, you aren't entitled to deny that there is a God; at best you can be an agnostic, taking no position on the question.

Many atheists, however, reject this burden of proof, maintaining that atheism is intellectually justified simply because there is no good case for theism—no line of argument that makes it reasonable to conclude that God exists. The extreme form of this response compares belief in God to belief in Santa Claus or the Easter Bunny—something we don't need to refute because there's obviously nothing to be said for it. Kitcher rightly rejects this response, since he knows that respected philosophers have put forward serious arguments for God's existence. But he still thinks that the case for theism falls so far short that atheism rather than agnosticism is the proper view to hold. A full discussion of whether atheists like Kitcher should instead be agnostics would lead us through a fascinating epistemological labyrinth (and my interview with Keith DeRose will explore the question a bit further).

Even if we could push Kitcher and others like him into the agnostic corner, they might nonetheless be agnostics utterly indifferent to belief in God. Theism might simply not be, to use William James's phrase, a "live option for him", something that he could envisage believing or even wanting to believe. For all practical purposes, this agnosticism would be no different from atheism. In the "Further Thoughts" to my interview with Daniel Garber, I propose a line of thought aimed at overcoming this "atheism of indifference".

6

RELIGION AND
SCIENTIFIC COSMOLOGY

(TIM MAUDLIN)

Cosmology—the attempt to understand the nature of the universe as a whole—developed in the earliest civilizations, and there is a continuous history of cosmological theories from Plato and Aristotle to the present. Throughout this history, we find ideas based on religious doctrines and philosophical reasoning, as well as empirical observation. With the invention of the telescope, empirical observation became the driving force behind enormous leaps forward in cosmology, and everyone knows about the early conflicts between the work of scientists such as Galileo and traditional religious ideas. But it is often forgotten that the new science of the universe produced at least as many arguments for religion as against. The more scientists learned about the precision with which an elegantly simple set of laws governed the entire universe, the more people—including most of the scientists involved—became convinced that these laws called for a divine creator.

The argument that connected the laws of nature to a creator God was typically expressed as an analogy between the natural world and the machines we make for various purposes. As Cleanthes, a character in Hume's *Dialogues Concerning Natural Religion*, puts it: "Look round the world: contemplate the whole and every part of it: you will find it to be nothing but one great machine, subdivided into an infinite number of lesser machines. . . . All these various machines, and even their most minute parts, are adjusted to each other with an accuracy which ravishes into admiration all men who have ever contemplated them. The curious adapting of means to ends, throughout all nature, resembles exactly, though it much exceeds, the productions of human contrivance; of human designs, thought, wisdom, and intelligence."

In the course of the discussion, Philo—an ingenious skeptic—raises a battery of objections aimed at undermining the conclusion that a divine intelligence must have contrived this natural order. But at the end of the *Dialogues*, Hume has Philo concede that the hypothesis of intelligent design is unavoidable: "A purpose, an intention, a design, strikes every where the most careless, the most stupid thinker; and no man can be so hardened in absurd systems, as at all times to reject it . . . and thus all the sciences almost lead us insensibly to acknowledge a first intelligent Author." Scholars dispute whether Philo represents Hume's own view or a prudent deferral to common opinion. But despite Laplace's famous insistence that his physics needed no such hypothesis, the design argument long made Newtonian science much more the friend than the enemy of theism.

Of course, all this began to change once Darwin postulated natural selection, the mechanism that promised a non-theistic explanation of the apparent design of organisms. (My interview with Michael Ruse will discuss the significance of this development.) Theists still urged the need to explain the very existence of the universe—including the mechanisms of evolution—as the creation of a supernatural being. Countering this, nonbelievers argued that the universe itself, existing back into infinite time, needed no supernatural explanation. Then, however, came the remarkable discovery of the Big Bang, suggesting that the universe had not always existed but originated in an "explosion", apparently from nothing, about fourteen billion years ago.

Tim Maudlin is a philosopher of science, specializing in the philosophy of physics, with particular emphasis on the theory of relativity and quantum physics. In our interview he argues that discoveries in scientific cosmology since the seventeenth century have refuted fundamental religious claims. He notes that monotheistic religious believers seldom rest with the minimal metaphysical claim that a divine being created the universe. They go on to claim that the human race has a central role in this creation—and is perhaps even the main purpose of creation. In Maudlin's view, this claim has been refuted by cosmology since Copernicus and Galileo, showing that our Earth is not the center of the universe, that our solar system has no privileged position among the billions of such systems in our galaxy, and that our galaxy itself has no central place in the universe as a whole. Similarly, in temporal terms, our Earth did not exist until ten billion years after the universe began, and human life appeared only billions of years after that. According to Maudlin, our marginal spatial and temporal position in the universe undermines any claim to our being the purpose of its creation.

In our discussion, I express some reservations about this view, and our disagreement seems to come down to the question of whether we have any basis for expecting that God would signal his special concern for us through our spatial or temporal place in the universe. Readers will, of course, draw their own conclusions.

Maudlin also discusses the cosmological argument for God's existence, based on the idea that nothing—and certainly not the entire universe—can come from nothing. A standard objection to the cosmological argument is that it ignores the possibility that the universe has always existed. As we've seen, believers have argued that Big Bang cosmology overcomes this objection since it specifies a precise past time at which the universe began to exist, thereby excluding its infinite past existence. But some physicists think current physics allows for a universe that came from nothing. Lawrence Krauss, for example, rejects the cosmological argument since, he says, its force depends on the meaning of "nothing" and, in the context of cosmology, this meaning in turn depends on what sense science can make of the term. For example, one plausible scientific meaning for "nothing" is "empty space": space with no elementary particles in it. But quantum mechanics, the long-established framework for understanding elementary particles, shows that they can emerge from empty space and so seems to show that the universe (that is, elementary particles and therefore the things they make up) *could* come from nothing.

Maudlin suggests that we don't currently have enough

scientific evidence to decide whether there's a plausible initial state from which the universe could have emerged. But he also maintains that there's no scientific evidence for divine creation, although he doesn't quite dismiss the possibility that someday such evidence might be found.

Big Bang physics has also seemed to give new life to the teleological argument, based on the idea that there are features of the universe that call for an intelligent designer. The Big Bang not only produced space, time, and matter, but also various constants corresponding to the "initial conditions" of the universe (its state right after the Big Bang). Various calculations are said to show that the values of these constants must lie within an extremely narrow range to allow for anything more than a chaotic universe that would never produce the complex and stable elements needed for the existence of organisms. Some scientists have joined philosophers and theologians in maintaining that these results show that the fundamental constants of the universe have been "fine-tuned" to allow the otherwise enormously improbable emergence of organic—in particular human—life. This "fine-tuning", they argue, must be the work of a divine intelligent designer of the universe.

But another development in recent cosmology has added another dimension to the discussion. String theory, the mathematical basis of some of the most promising recent work on cosmology, may allow for the possibility that the Big Bang produced (by a process of "inflation") not just our universe but an infinite number of independently existing universes, each perhaps with its own set of laws of nature and values for their fundamental constants. If this were so, then there would be nothing puzzling about there being one universe (ours) fine-tuned for life. It's important to note that this "multiverse" possibility was not put forward to defeat the fine-tuning argument for theism. It was suggested by independent calculations derived from the mathematics of string theory.

Maudlin argues that we simply don't know enough about the scientific status of the "constants" (if that's what they are) to support the claims of the fine-tuning argument. But he also maintains that the inflation and multiverse hypotheses likewise remain highly speculative and so can't exclude possible fine-tuning arguments.

INTERVIEW WITH TIM MAUDLIN*

Gary Gutting: Could you begin by noting aspects of recent scientific cosmology that are particularly relevant to theological questions?

Tim Maudlin: That depends on the given theological account. The biblical account of the origin of the cosmos in Genesis, for example, posits that a god created the physical universe particularly with human beings in mind, and so unsurprisingly placed the Earth at the center of creation.

Modern cosmological knowledge has refuted such an account. We are living in the golden age of cosmology: More has been discovered about the large-scale

---

* This interview was originally published as "Modern Cosmology Versus God's Creation" in *The Stone* (blog), *New York Times,* June 15, 2014.

structure and history of the visible cosmos in the last twenty years than in the whole of prior human history. We now have precise knowledge of the distribution of galaxies and know that ours is nowhere near the center of the universe, just as we know that our planetary system has no privileged place among the billions of such systems in our galaxy and that Earth is not even at the center of our planetary system. We also know that the Big Bang, the beginning of our universe, occurred about 13.7 billion years ago, whereas Earth didn't even exist until about 10 billion years later.

No one looking at the vast extent of the universe and the completely random location of *Homo sapiens* within it (in both space and time) could seriously maintain that the whole thing was intentionally created for us. This realization began with Galileo, and has only intensified ever since.

G.G.: I don't see why the extent of the universe and our nonprivileged spatiotemporal position within it says anything about whether we have some special role in the universe. The major monotheistic religions maintain that there is a special *spiritual* relationship between us and the creator. But that doesn't imply that this is the only purpose of the universe or that we're the only creatures with a special relationship to the creator.

T.M.: Yes, of course, there are, in theory, other possible hypotheses about the origin of the universe and our role in it. Someone might hold that the universe was created with humans playing some important role, but a role equally played by other living beings (not living on Earth); or that the universe was created with some living beings playing an important role, but that humans are not among them; or even that the universe was created with no particular regard for any living beings.

If cosmology is to bear on any such hypothesis, then the hypothesis must lead to some expectations for the sort of universe a deity so motivated would create. The expectations following from the accounts, such as Genesis, that make us the main purpose of the universe have, as I've pointed out, the great weight of evidence against them. (The other sorts of hypotheses have not been much advocated to my knowledge, and hence not developed to the point where one would know what sort of a physical universe to expect if any of them were true. My guess is that most religious people would not be especially interested in these hypotheses.)

G.G.: I think we need to distinguish different sorts of theism. There are versions of theism that, like a literal reading of Genesis, are inconsistent with what we know about cosmology. But there are also versions that don't require any specific story about the extent of the physical universe or our location in it. For example, there's a basic theism that merely asserts that there's an intelligent being that created the entire universe. It says nothing about what the purpose of God's creation was, beyond simply making a universe. So I don't see why every version of theism is refuted by scientific cosmology.

T.M.: Theism, as religious people typically hold it, does not merely state that some entity created the universe, but that the universe was created specifically with humans in mind as the most important part of creation. If we have any understanding at all of how an intelligent agent capable of creating the material universe would act if it had such an intention, we would say it would not create the huge structure we see, most of it completely irrelevant for life on Earth, with the Earth in such a seemingly random location, and with humans appearing only after a long and rather random course of evolution.

G.G.: Maybe, but that conclusion doesn't follow from scientific cosmology; it's based on further assumptions about what a creator would want—and how the creator would go about achieving it. Moreover, theistic religions can allow for many other intelligent creatures with a special relation to God; and it's even plausible to think that God might have made a huge and complex universe as an object of knowledge for intelligent creatures. From that standpoint, the development of scientific cosmology would be part of God's plan.

In any case, I'd like to hear your thoughts on a recent effort to find scientific support for religious views. Some theists have appealed to scientific cosmology to argue that there's a "fine-tuning" of physical constants that shows that the universe is designed to support living beings and, in particular, humans. It's said, for example, that if the ratio of the mass of the neutron to the mass of the proton were just slightly different, there couldn't be sufficient structure to allow for the existence of organisms like us.

T.M.: At this point, our physical theories contain quite a large number of "constants of nature", of which we have no deeper account. There seem to be more of them than most physicists are comfortable with, and we don't know for sure whether these "constants" are really constant rather than variable. This gives rise to questions about "fine-tuning" of these constants. One thing to keep in mind is that the true number and status of the "constants of nature" is not part of any well-established physical theory: It is part of what we don't yet know rather than what we do know.

G.G.: So are you saying that we don't know enough about the relevant constants to get a theistic argument started?

T.M.: Yes, since we don't even know if the "constants" are constant, we certainly don't know enough to draw any conclusions about the best account of why they have the particular values they have right now and around here. Since we don't know how the various "constants" might be related to each other by deeper physics, the game of trying to figure out the effect of changing just one and leaving the rest alone also is not well founded.

One thing is for sure: If there were some deity who desired that we know of its existence, there would be simple, clear ways to convey that information. I would say that any theistic argument that starts with the constants of nature cannot end with a deity who is interested in us knowing of its existence.

G.G.: Once again, that's assuming we are good judges of how the deity would behave. But suppose that a surprisingly narrow range of the relevant constants turns out to be necessary for humans to exist. Some critics would say that even so, cosmological inflation would provide a satisfactory explanation with no reference to a creator. What's your view on that?

T.M.: Not everything about cosmology is known. We do not know how to reconcile quantum theory and relativity yet, and such a reconciliation would be needed to investigate the nature of the Big Bang. In particular, we don't understand the basic physics well enough to tell if anything preceded the Big Bang. Even the existence of an inflationary period is still controversial.

One very speculative idea in cosmology is that the entire universe contains infinitely many "pocket universes" or "bubble universes", in each of which the quantities we call "constants of nature" take different, randomly chosen, values. If so, then every possible combination of such values occurs somewhere, and living beings will obviously only evolve in regions where the combination of values supports life. Such an account predicts that intelligent creatures would arise in essentially random locations in a huge cosmological structure, just as we see.

But this idea is highly speculative, and there is no direct evidence in its favor.

G.G.: So is your view that we don't currently know enough to decide whether or not fine-tuning for human life supports theism?

T.M.: First, note how "humans" got put into that question! If there were any argument like this to be made, it would go through equally well for cockroaches. They too can only exist in certain physical conditions. The attempt to put *Homo sapiens* at the center of this discussion is a reflection of our egocentrism, and has no basis at all in the actual structure of the universe.

Consider a different hypothesis: Suppose that there is a deity who created the universe with particular attention to the fate of some creatures in a distant galaxy. The very existence of the Earth and the evolution of life on Earth was just an unintended by-product of setting up the "constants of nature" for the sake of those creatures, not us. That would be a fascinating thing to find out, but not what most people with interests in theism were after. The actual values of the "constants of nature" certainly cannot provide *more* evidence for their (Genesis-like) hypothesis than for this hypothesis.

G.G.: Finally, let me ask about what I've called causal theism, which merely argues that a creator is needed to explain the very existence of the universe, regardless of its purpose. Some cosmologists, like Lawrence Krauss, have suggested that current physical theory shows how the universe could have emerged from nothing—for example, by a quantum fluctuation. What do you think of this suggestion?

T.M.: The more general claim that a creator is needed to explain the very existence of the universe is a much, much weaker claim, and is consistent with humanity having had no particular significance at all to the creator. That's why I say that just getting some creator or other is not what most people are after.

In any case, does there need to be a nonmaterial cause as an explanation for the entire material universe? Causal explanation either goes on forever backward in time or it comes to a stop somewhere. Even people who want to postulate a nonmaterial cause of the material universe often see no need to invoke yet another cause for that nonmaterial cause, and so are content to let the sequence of causal explanations come to an end. But the initial state of the universe (if there is one) could just as well be the uncaused cause. Or if there is no initial state, and the universe goes back infinitely in time, then it can't have a cause that precedes it in time.

Krauss does not suggest that the universe came to exist "from nothing" in the sense of "did not come from anything at all", but rather that it came from a quantum vacuum state. He seems to think that such a vacuum state would be a satisfying place to end the causal regress as the state with no causal antecedent. The vacuum state has many important symmetries, so if one could tell a physical story of everything coming out of a vacuum state, it would have a certain appealing plausibility. But one could still ask, "Why start with the vacuum state rather than something else?" I think we don't know enough to make any plausible guess about even whether there was an initial state, much less what it might have been. This goes beyond what we have good evidence or theory for.

G.G.: You obviously don't see scientific cosmology as supporting any case for theism. You also think that it refutes theistic religions' claiming that the primary purpose of God's creation is the existence of human beings. What, finally, is your view about the minimal theistic view that the universe was created by an intelligent being (regardless of its purpose)? Does scientific cosmology support the atheistic position that there is no such creator or does it leave us with the agnostic judgment that there isn't sufficient evidence to say?

T.M.: Atheism is the default position in any scientific inquiry, just as aquarkism or aneutrinoism was. That is, any entity has to earn its admission into a scientific account either via direct evidence for its existence or because it plays some fundamental explanatory role. Before the theoretical need for neutrinos was appreciated (to preserve the conservation of energy) and then later experimental detection was made, they were not part of the accepted physical account of the world. To say physicists in 1900 were "agnostic" about neutrinos sounds wrong: they just did not believe there were such things.

As yet, there is no direct experimental evidence of a deity, and in order for the postulation of a deity to play an explanatory role there would have to be a lot of detail about how it would act. If, as you have suggested, we are not "good judges of how the deity would behave", then such an unknown and unpredictable deity cannot provide good explanatory grounds for any phenomenon. The problem with the "minimal view" is that in trying to be as vague as possible about the nature and motivation of the deity, the hypothesis loses any explanatory force, and so cannot be admitted on scientific grounds. Of course, as the example of quarks and neutrinos shows, scientific accounts change in response to new data and new theory. The default position can be overcome.

FURTHER THOUGHTS

Maudlin's discussion of Krauss's claim that science might show how something could come from nothing raises further philosophical issues that are worth discussing. Krauss admits that particles can emerge from empty space because empty space, despite its name, does contain fields (called "virtual fields") that fluctuate and "spontaneously" produce particles. A critic may well urge that these virtual fields are the "something" from which the particles come. But to this Krauss can respond that there is a further possibility: the long-sought quantum theory of gravity, uniting quantum mechanics and general relativity, may allow for the spontaneous production of empty space itself, simply by virtue of the theory's laws. Then everything—space, fields, and particles—could come from nothing.

But, the critic may persist, what about the theory's laws? They are something, not nothing—and where do they come from? At this point it might seem that there's no way Krauss can win this battle. At every turn, the physicist's account presupposes the existence of something (particles, fields, laws, a multiverse—whatever). In no case, then, does something really come from nothing.

But perhaps the critic is winning the battle yet losing the war. There is an absolute use of "nothing" that excludes literally everything that exists. In one sense, Krauss is obstinately ignoring this use. He seems to assume that "coming from nothing" means "coming from a preexisting state in which nothing exists", whereas it means "coming into existence from no preexisting state". But he could readily cite philosophers who find this absolute use—and the corresponding principle that something cannot come from nothing—unintelligible, impossible to understand. Henri Bergson, for example, argued that when we claim something doesn't exist, it must be because something else exists in a way that excludes it. There is no one sitting in this chair because everyone is somewhere else. There has never been an American president under the age of thirty-five because the Constitution forbids it.

If Bergson is right, the idea of a state in which nothing at all exists is unintelligible; it violates the condition that non-existence is always a function of what exists. We need to distinguish our ordinary use of "nothing" as relative (to what exists) from an unintelligible use of "nothing" as an absolute (a state in which absolutely nothing exists). If we do this, we will realize that the question *Can something come from nothing?* is meaningless if it takes "nothing" as an absolute. But if what "nothing" means depends on context, cosmology may be able to tell us what, in the context of the universe as a whole, "nothing" means.

We may have our doubts about Bergson's argument. But even if the claim survives philosophical critiques of its intelligibility, there are still objections to applying "something cannot come from nothing" to the universe as a whole. David Hume, for example, argued in his *Dialogues* that it is only from experience that we know that individual things don't just spring into existence (saying that they do so is not a logical contradiction, so it is not strictly impossible). Since we have no experience of the universe coming into existence, we have no reason to say that if it has come to be, it must have a cause.

7

Religion and Evolution

(MICHAEL RUSE)

Michael Ruse is a leading philosopher of biology and, in particular, an expert on Charles Darwin. For more than a century, Darwin's account of evolution by natural selection has been the strongest scientific challenge to religious belief. Its most decisive victory has been the refutation of creationist claims that Earth and the life on it originated only a few thousand years ago. These claims now lie in the junkyard of intellectual history. But many scientifically informed thinkers also maintain that evolution undermines the very idea of a creator god.

As Richard Dawkins puts it, theism seems at least plausible if we think the only alternatives for explaining our impressively complex universe are chance and design. As we've seen, even a skeptic like David Hume found it hard to see how this impressive "machine" could have come about just by accident. But, Dawkins points out, Darwin discovered a third way: natural selection combined with chance can, given enough time, explain any degree of the complexity we might otherwise attribute to a designer.

Darwin explained the development of more complex organisms through a series of small chance changes that start from much simpler organisms. When a small change (a new trait) is both hereditary (passed on to offspring genetically) and adaptive (provides an advantage that makes for having more offspring), subsequent generations will have more and more individuals with the trait and eventually all individuals will have the trait. Over long periods of time, many such small changes can lead to organisms far more complex than their remote ancestors. So, for example, a light-sensitive spot could, through many small steps, develop into an eye.

This general framework, however, does not by itself guarantee an explanation of a specific major biological change. To produce a specific explanation we need two things: first, particular small changes (mutations), all both hereditary and adaptive, that will eventually produce the major change; second, enough time for the series to result in the major change. This, some maintain, provides an opening for a theistic counter to the Darwinian challenge: the theory of "intelligent design", which accepts evolution but maintains that there are aspects of the process that we can satisfactorily explain only by assuming the intervention of an intelligent designer (God).

Proponents of intelligent design present it as a rival scientific account, pointing to various cases in which evolutionary biologists have not found a series of changes that would have produced the change in the time available. The human eye is one favorite example, but other traits such as blood clotting and the immune system are also cited.

Intelligent design is, therefore, based on what it sees as the failure of evolutionary theory to provide satisfactory explanations of how certain organisms evolved. There's no denying that there are many cases for which we do not—and for all practical purposes never will—have anything close to a detailed account of how a given trait evolved. The same is true in all branches of science. We do not have detailed accounts of the immensely complex processes that produce hurricanes, earthquakes, or stars. The question is not whether such accounts have been given but whether there is good reason to think that they could, in principle, be given. Isn't it reasonable to think that with enough detailed information evolutionary biologists could describe the overall process that produced the eye, blood clotting, and so on? Don't the many detailed evolutionary accounts that we do have show that the theory is at least a good approximation of the truth and so should apply to all cases?

We may think this is too strong a claim, that no scientific theory is so well established that we should expect it to hold up indefinitely. After all, hasn't the history of science been, as Thomas Kuhn argued, the history of scientific revolutions, with even, for example, Newtonian physics eventually yielding to the radically new conceptions of relativity and quantum theory? So why couldn't intelligent design be a candidate to replace evolutionary theory?

But suppose that scientists do conclude that the theory of evolution as we now have it is fundamentally inadequate. What reason would they have for moving to intelligent design as opposed to an alternative that didn't posit a superhuman intelligence?

In looking to replace a failed theory, scientists are looking for an account that will do two things: (1) explain at least most of what the old theory explained while also explaining the phenomena the old theory failed to explain, and (2) successfully predict new phenomena. Scientists need theories that not only account for what we already know but also suggest new hypotheses that they can test. But there is no way for an intelligent-design theory to provide new hypotheses, since we have no basis for knowing how an intelligence far beyond our own would have designed the world. To drive this point home, do a thought experiment suggested by David Hume in his *Dialogues*: think of the ideal world you would create if you had the power—and notice how different it is from the world we actually have. We can, of course, always consistently explain any gap in a Darwinian (or other purely natural) account of evolution by assuming the intervention of a supernatural intelligence. But what basis would we have for predicting new phenomena that were due to this intelligence? Given the enormous superiority of this intelligence to our own, we would seem to have no basis for any such predictions. In any case, proponents of intelligent design have not produced any successful prediction based on their theory. Therefore, intelligent design does not offer a serious scientific supplement to evolution.

Ruse has been a major critic of intelligent design, both in his writing and as an expert witness in highly publicized lawsuits over teaching evolution in public schools. Here he was on the side of Richard Dawkins, himself a notable biologist, and, like Ruse, an atheist. But as we will see, Ruse's atheism has a very different character from Dawkins's atheism.

The difference shows up especially in Ruse's view of the claim that there is no God because there's no place for the supernatural in our scientific account of the world. This claim supports atheism only if we add the further claim that science is the only way of knowing what there is. Although Ruse identifies himself as an atheist, he thinks that there are questions about what is real that science cannot answer and that religion might, in principle, be able to answer. This is because science always bases its explanations on what Ruse calls a "mechanical" model (or metaphor): it posits certain realities that are used to explain things we observe. This, he points out, at least makes science incapable of answering the question "Why are there any realities at all?" or, as philosophers usually put it, "Why is there something rather than nothing?"

We've seen that Henri Bergson thought this question makes no sense, and various analytic philosophers have agreed. Ruse, however, agrees with philosophers such as Aquinas, Leibniz, and Heidegger, who think the question is both intelligible and important. But even if we think it makes no sense to ask why there's something rather than nothing, it does make sense to ask whether there's something that's beyond the reach of scientific knowledge. By definition, science can't answer this question. Science, like any other mode of inquiry (mathematics, for example) cannot answer questions about what might exist beyond its domain of knowledge. Nonetheless, Ruse rejects God as the answer to the question of why anything at all exists because he cannot reconcile a good and powerful God with the evil he sees in the world.

INTERVIEW WITH MICHAEL RUSE*

Gary Gutting: What do you think of the claim that scientific accounts provide all the explanations needed to understand the existence and nature of the world, so that there's no need to posit God as the ultimate explanation?

Michael Ruse: Let me start at a more general level by saying that I don't think science as such can explain everything. Therefore, assuming that the existence and nature of the world can be fully understood (I'm not sure it can!), this is going to require something more than science. As far as I am concerned, if you want God to have a crack at the job, go right ahead!

G.G.: Could you say a bit more about why you think that science can't fully explain everything?

M.R.: In my view none of our knowledge, including science, just "tells it like it is". Knowledge, even the best scientific knowledge, interprets experience through human cultural understanding and experience, and above all (just as it is for poets and preachers) metaphor is the key to the whole enterprise. As I developed my own career path, as a historian and philosopher of evolutionary biology, this insight grew and grew.

* This interview was originally published as "Does Evolution Explain Religious Beliefs?" in *The Stone* (blog), *New York Times,* July 8, 2014.

Everything was metaphorical—struggle for existence, natural selection, division of labor, genetic code, arms races, and more.

G.G.: It's clear that metaphors are useful when scientists try to explain complex ideas in terms nonscientists can understand, but why think they have an essential role in the development of scientific knowledge?

M.R.: Because metaphor helps you move forward. It is heuristic, forcing you to ask new questions. If your love is like a rose, what color is the rose? But note that it does so at a cost. A metaphor puts blinkers on us. Some questions are unanswerable within the context of the metaphor. "My love is a rose" tells me about her beauty. It does not tell me about her mathematical abilities.

Now combine this fact with history. Since the scientific revolution one metaphor above all—the root metaphor—has dictated the nature and progress of science. This is the metaphor of the world as a machine: the mechanical metaphor. What questions are ruled out by this metaphor? One is about ultimate origins. Of course you can ask about the origins of the metal and plastics in your automobile, but ultimately the questions must end and you must take the materials as given. So with the world. I think the machine metaphor rules out an answer to what Martin Heidegger called the "fundamental question of metaphysics": Why is there something rather than nothing? Unlike Wittgenstein, I think it is a genuine question, but not one answerable by modern science.

Coming now to my own field of evolutionary biology, I see some questions that it simply doesn't ask but that can be asked and answered by other areas of science. I think here about the natural origins of the universe and the Big Bang theory. I see some questions that it doesn't ask and that neither it nor any other science can answer. One such question is why there is something rather than nothing or, if you like, why ultimately there are material substances from which organisms are formed.

G.G.: So do you think that we need religion to answer the ultimate question of the world's origin?

M.R.: If the person of faith wants to say that God created the world, I don't think you can deny this on scientific grounds. But you can go after the theist on other grounds. I would raise philosophical objections: for example, about the notion of a necessary being. I would also fault Christian theology: I don't think you can mesh the Greek notion of a god outside time and space with the Jewish notion of a god as a person. But these are not scientific objections.

G.G.: What do you think of Richard Dawkins's argument that, in any case, God won't do as an ultimate explanation of the universe? His point is that complexity requires explanation—the whole idea of evolution by natural selection is to explain the origin of complex life forms from less-complex life forms. But a creator God—with enormous knowledge and power—would have to be at least as complex as the universe he creates. Such a creator would require explanation by something else and so couldn't explain, for example, why there's something rather than nothing.

M.R.: Like every first-year undergraduate in philosophy, Dawkins thinks he can put to rest the causal argument for God's existence. If God caused the world, then what caused God? Of course, the great philosophers, Anselm and Aquinas particularly, are way ahead of him here. They know that the only way to stop the regression is by making God something that needs no cause. He must be a necessary being. This means that God is not part of the regular causal chain but in some sense orthogonal to it. He is what keeps the whole business going, past, present and future, and is the explanation of why there is something rather than nothing. Also God is totally simple, and I don't see why complexity should not arise out of this, just as it does in mathematics and science from very simple premises.

Traditionally God's necessity is not logical necessity but some kind of metaphysical necessity, or aseity. Unlike Hume, I don't think this is a silly or incoherent idea, any more than I think mathematical Platonism is silly or incoherent. As it happens, I am not a mathematical Platonist, and I do have conceptual difficulties with the idea of metaphysical necessity. So in the end, I am not sure that the Christian God idea flies, but I want to extend to Christians the courtesy of arguing against what they actually believe, rather than begin and end with the polemical parody of what Dawkins calls "the God delusion".

G.G.: Do you think that evolution lends support to the atheistic argument from evil: that it makes no sense to think that an all-good, all-powerful God would have used so wasteful and brutal a process as evolution to create living things?

M.R.: Although I know that in some philosophy of religion circles it is now thought that we can counter the argument from evil, I don't think this is so. More than that, I don't want it to be so. I don't want an argument that convinces me that the death under the guillotine of Sophie Scholl (one of the leaders of the White Rose group opposed to the Nazis) or of Anne Frank in Bergen-Belsen ultimately contributes to the greater good. If my eternal salvation depends on the deaths of these two young women, then forget it.

This said, I have never really thought that the pains brought on by the evolutionary process, in particular the struggle for survival and reproduction, much affect the Christian conception of God. For all of Voltaire's devastating wit in *Candide*, I am a bit of a Leibnizian on these matters. If God is to do everything through unbroken law, and I can think of good theological reasons why this should be so, then pain and suffering is part of it all. Paradoxically and humorously I am with Dawkins here. He argues that the only natural way you can get the design-like features of organisms—the hand

and the eye—is through evolution by natural selection, brought on by the struggle. Other mechanisms just don't work. So God is off the hook.

G.G.: What do you think of the claim that evolutionary accounts show that religion emerged not because of any evidence for its truth but because of its adaptive value?

M.R.: It is interesting that you ask this question, because recently I've found myself wrestling with this issue more than just about any other. As an ardent Darwinian evolutionist I think that all organisms, and I include us humans, are the end product of a long, slow process of development thanks to the causal mechanism of natural selection. So this means that I think features like the eye and the hand are around because of their adaptive value; they help us to survive and reproduce.

G.G.: Of course, evolutionary explanations are empirically well established on the biological level. But is the same true on the level of social and cultural life, especially among humans?

M.R.: I include society and culture here although I would qualify what I say. I don't see being a Nazi as being very adaptive, but I would say that the things that lead to being a Nazi—for instance being open to indoctrination as a child—have adaptive significance. I would say the same of religion. The biologist Edward O. Wilson thinks that religion is adaptive because it promotes bonding and he might be right. But it can go biologically haywire, as in the case of the Shakers, whose religious prohibition on procreation had an adaptive value of precisely zero.

So it is true that in a sense I see all knowledge, including claims about religious knowledge, as being relative to evolutionary ends. The upshot is that I don't dismiss religious beliefs even though they ultimately can be explained by evolution. I think everything can! I wouldn't dismiss religious beliefs even if you could show me that they are just a by-product of adaptation, as I think Darwin himself thought. It is as plausible that my love of Mozart's operas is a by-product of adaptation, but it doesn't make them any the less beautiful and meaningful. I think you have to judge religion on its merits.

G.G.: Is one of religion's merits that it provides a foundation (intellectual and practical) for morality through the idea of God as divine lawgiver?

M.R.: I am on record as an "evolutionary skeptic". I don't deny substantive morality—you ought to return your library books on time—but I do deny objective foundations. I think morality is a collective illusion, genetic in origin, that makes us good cooperators. And I would add that being good cooperators makes each one of us individually better off in the struggle for existence. If we are nice to other people, they are much more likely to be nice to us in return. However, as the philosopher

J. L. Mackie used to argue, I think we "objectify" substantive ethics—we think it objectively the case that we
ought to return library books on time. But we do this
(or rather our genes make us do this) because if we
didn't we would all start to cheat and substantive ethics
would collapse to the ground.

So I don't buy the moral argument for the existence
of God. I think you can have all of the morality you need
without God. I am a follower of Hume brought up to
date by Darwin. Morality is purely emotions, although
emotions of a special kind with an important adaptive
function. I don't, however, think that here I am necessarily denying the existence of God. Were I a Christian,
I would be somewhat of a natural law theorist, thinking that morality is what is natural. Caring about small
children is natural and good; killing small children for
laughs is unnatural and bad. If you want to say that God
created the world and what is good therefore is what fits
with the way God designed it, I am OK with this. In fact,
I think you should say it to avoid the problem (raised in
Plato's *Euthyphro*) of simply making the good a function
of God's arbitrary will.

G.G.: There seems to be a tension in your thinking about
religion. You aren't yourself a believer, but you spend a
great deal of time defending belief against its critics.

M.R.: People often accuse me of being self-contradictory, if not of outright hypocrisy. I won't say I accept
the ontological argument for the existence of God—

the argument that derives God's existence from his essence—but I do like it (it is so clever) and I am prepared to stand up for it when Dawkins dismisses it with scorn rather than good reasons. In part this is a turf war. I am a professional philosopher. I admire immensely thinkers like Anselm and Descartes and am proud to be one of them, however minor and inadequate in comparison. I am standing up for my own. In part, this is political. Religion is a big thing in America, and often not a very good big thing. I don't think you are going to counter the bad just by going over the top, like in the Battle of the Somme. I think you have to reach out over no-man's-land to the trenches on the other side and see where we can agree and hope to move forward.

I should say that my Quaker childhood—as in everything I do and think—is tremendously important here. I grew up surrounded by gentle, loving (and very intelligent) Christians. I never forget that. Finally, I just don't like bad arguments. In my case, I think I can offer good arguments against the existence of the Christian God. I don't need the inadequate and faulty. In "Murder in the Cathedral," T. S. Eliot has Thomas à Becket say: "The last temptation is the greatest treason: To do the right deed for the wrong reason." Amen.

FURTHER THOUGHTS:
AN EVOLUTIONARY ARGUMENT FOR ATHEISM

My interview with Ruse touched briefly on Dawkins's evolutionary argument for atheism. Here I formulate the argument more fully and discuss Ruse's appeal to metaphysical concepts of God to respond to it.

It seems clear that evolution provides a satisfactory explanation of the apparent design of the universe. Biological evolution admittedly explains only the origin of complex life-forms from simpler life-forms, but it is highly likely that physics and chemistry will develop their own evolutionary accounts, parallel to those of biology. What need, then, is there for the theistic hypothesis? But pointing out that God is not needed to explain design merely shows that theist arguments from design are unsuccessful. It doesn't show that there is no God, and there might be other (nonscientific) reasons for thinking that there is—for example, metaphysical arguments (cosmological, ontological), moral arguments, or arguments from religious experience.

But Dawkins suggests an argument that offers a stronger challenge to theism. Both those who argue for God through the design argument and those who argue against the design argument through evolution agree that complex structures (things made up of various elements all working together) require an explanation. Any being capable of designing and creating the universe must itself be highly complex. For example, it must know many things and have the ability to produce a wide variety of effects. But this complexity itself requires explanation. (By contrast, natural selection produces more complex systems from simpler systems.) But the divine creator is claimed to *be* the ultimate explanation and therefore cannot itself *require* explanation. Since the creator does require explanation, it cannot be the ultimate explanation.

In our interview, Ruse rightly points out that this line of

argument ignores the traditional theological view that God is simple (not a combination of various properties) and necessary (existing no matter what, and so requiring no explanation). But simplicity and necessity are very peculiar features. If God is simple, then what seem to be his different properties are actually the same property; for example, his justice and his mercy must be identical, as must his love of virtue and his hatred of vice. In fact, God can have only one property (which we might call total greatness) and there can't be any difference between God and that property. Therefore, God must be nothing but a property and not something that has properties. But then God could not be a person who has properties such as creating us, loving us, and offering us a chance for eternal salvation.

As to necessary existence, the only things that seem to have this status are mathematical or logical abstractions such as numbers or principles of reasoning, which are a far cry from persons of any sort. Further, God is supposed to be perfect, so that if he exists necessarily, then he is necessarily perfect, which would mean that he is, among other things, always entirely happy (surely a very important perfection). But how could such a God love us? How, for example, could he be just as happy when we return his love as when we reject it? The appeal to divine simplicity and necessity may avoid the need to explain God, but it makes it extraordinarily difficult to identify such a being with the God most people believe in.

This abstruse metaphysical discussion of God may seem far removed from anything that interests most believers. But in fact it reveals a fundamental tension in monotheistic religions. On the one hand, they need God to be the ultimate creative source of the universe, not just another thing in the universe. But this requires thinking of him in terms of metaphysical abstractions like simplicity and necessity, since otherwise his existence will have to depend on something else. This is why theologians have developed metaphysical systems based on the work of philosophers such as Plato and Aristotle to discuss the nature of God. But, on the other hand, the God of the Bible is obviously a person, interacting with human beings and sharing—although to a higher degree—human characteristics such as love, sorrow, and delight. This tension between "Athens and Jerusalem" seems essential to the self-understanding of monotheistic religions.

8

A MUSLIM PERSPECTIVE

(SAJJAD RIZVI)

There is a venerable distinction, going back at least to the Middle Ages, between *natural religion* and *revealed religion*. Natural religion is said to be based on sound rational arguments for the existence and the nature of a divine being. Religion in this sense is an obvious concern of philosophy and is also the field on which contemporary theists and atheists engage. It's no surprise, then, that these interviews mostly focus on natural religion. But for most of history, there has been general agreement about the existence of some sort of divine being or beings. Disputes—at least among Western monotheisms—have focused on which, if any, religion could claim the authority of a divine revelation: a direct intervention of God into history to tell us what he expects by way of belief and behavior. The teachings of any such revelation are not in general accessible to human reason but are reached through faith in the reliability of what an all-good and all-knowing God has told us.

A religion based on divine revelation in some ways sim-
plifies the justification of religious claims. There is no need
to make a separate case establishing the truth of every claim
made in, say, the Nicene Creed. Believers need not offer historical evidence for the Virgin Birth and the Resurrection
of Jesus; metaphysical proofs that God is triune and that the
Holy Spirit proceeds not just from the Father but from both
the Father and the Son; or moral arguments that we need to
have our sins forgiven and to offer God adoration and praise.
They establish such claims simply by pointing out that they
are among the truths God has revealed to us. Taking this
approach, religious faith may present itself as not an irrational leap but rather a sensible belief on the basis of an eminently reliable authority, no different in principle from the
way most of us believe scientific and historical claims on the
authority of experts.

There remains, of course, the question of whether in fact
there has been a divine revelation and, if there has, where we
can find it. On pain of logical circularity, this question cannot
be answered by an appeal to divine revelation, any more than
the pope can establish his infallibility by noting that he has
proclaimed that he is infallible. One traditional method of
showing that God has revealed a religion is to point to miracles performed by those who claim to have received the revelation. Here the idea is that a miracle requires divine power
and that God would not exercise this power to support a false-
hood. (Defending the divine origin of Christianity, Thomas
Aquinas responds to the suggestion that the alleged Christian
miracles might not have occurred by saying that, if so, the
widespread acceptance of so demanding a religion without

miracles would itself be the greatest of miracles.) Another traditional appeal—much more popular today than appeals to miracles—is to believers' direct insight into the divine origin of a book such as the Bible or the Quran.

But even if we accept, in principle, the possibility of a rational case for a divine revelation, there remains the undeniable fact that there are conflicting claims—from Jews, Christians, and Muslims, not to mention opposing sects within each religion—over who has received the true revelation. Moreover, even among those who agree that they have the revealed truth, there are interminable and often bitter disputes about what the truth means. We soon realize that, even if we knew for certain that a particular text or oral tradition contained all the important truths, this knowledge would not allow us to understand what it says.

My interview with Sajjad Rizvi, a Muslim and a distinguished scholar of Islam, illustrates all these issues in a concrete way. Rizvi presents Islam as a religion historically parallel to Christianity and Judaism that develops similar philosophical, theological, and cultural resources in very different ways but with equal detail, rigor, and sophistication.

INTERVIEW WITH SAJJAD RIZVI*

Gary Gutting: How do you see Islam in relation to the other major Abrahamic religions, Christianity and Judaism? Should we think of them as (for example) rivals, or

---

* This interview was originally published as "How Does Islam Relate to Christianity and Judaism?" in *The Stone* (blog), *New York Times*, September 25, 2014.

as complementary developments of monotheism, or as different cultural expressions of an essentially similar religious experience?

Sajjad Rizvi: The very notion of Abrahamic religions is arguably Islamic. The Quran presents Abraham as an adherent of Islam, but here "Islam" means the primordial faith that connects humanity to one God and leads in turn to Judaism, Christianity, and then historical Islam as proclaimed by Muhammad. There are some who view Islam as a faith that supersedes the two earlier monotheistic religions. But I think it's more useful to understand Islam as a religion that is self-conscious about its relationship to Judaism and Christianity and explicitly takes account of their scriptures and traditions. Almost all the prophets of the Quran will be familiar to those who know the Bible, and the Quran explicitly refers to parables, ideas, and stories from the Bible.

The common roots—and inheritances—of the three faiths make it useful for us to think seriously in terms of a Judeo-Christian-Islamic civilization and heritage that we all share. The development of philosophy in Islam also shows a common tradition of rationality. Anyone with a basic understanding of the categories of Aristotle's thought employed by Christian and Jewish thinkers would find many of the arguments of Islamic philosophers and theologians familiar. The great Islamic philosopher Avicenna (tenth to eleventh century) developed a metaphysical notion of God that had a tremendous impact on the Latin west: the idea that God is the necessary being required to explain the existence of every contingent being.

G.G.: But even given these deep similarities, doesn't Islam claim that the other two faiths are, if not entirely false, still not the full truth that Islam is?

S.R.: Ultimately, the Islamic reflection on the other two faiths considers them to be earlier versions and revelations of the same truth even if the long history from their sacral origins might have diluted their understanding. The Quran itself engages in a polemic with some of those communities often precisely because of the exclusive claims that they made about salvation. The Quran tends to insist upon God's final decision (to which we, of course, are not privy) against the presumptions of theologians. The fundamental distinctions in the scripture are between monotheistic believers, imperfect monotheists, and others: Jewish and Christian communities were considered often to be in the second category. Some theologians would consider them to be paler reflections of their original revelation—and some say that their scriptures have been corrupted. But we should not lose sight of how the Islamic tradition itself often refers back to the earlier Jewish and Christian scriptures and prophets to make sense of the mission of Muhammad.

G.G.: What about the fundamental question of salvation—do you go to heaven or go to hell? Does Islam say—as Christianity often has—that you can't be saved if you don't accept it? Or can, for example, Christians be saved?

S.R.: It depends on whom one reads. There's a whole range of opinions. The early scriptural traditions (especially in the Quran itself) are quite clear that success in the afterlife—everlasting life in paradise in the presence of God—is not exclusive to those who define themselves as Muslims in the historical sense. Belief in God and the afterlife and performing good deeds are the only conditions of success. Later theological traditions have complicated matters, but even then a tradition developed of considering punishment in hellfire to be not eternal, so that ultimately everyone will be embraced by God's mercy.

G.G.: Christianity and Islam are both religions that originated in specific cultural contexts but have developed into world religions, practiced by people in a wide variety of cultures. How would you compare or contrast their development in this regard?

S.R.: Christianity and Islam share the paradox of being religions that claim to be universal while retaining particular dogmas and practices that are exclusive to them. There were times when pursuit of world empire led both religions to more universal claims. Their trajectories seem similar—a small, persecuted faith that acquired an imperial form and expression that led to its dominance across the world. Here both used orthodoxy to bolster the authority of the empire, and defined heterodoxy to deal with political dissent. One of the main differences that has always struck me concerns how orthodoxy was shaped and implemented. On the whole, the Muslim world did not have the same mechanisms of central control—councils, creeds, and inquisitions—to enforce matters. They sometimes tried to set up such mechanisms, but always failed. When people raise the problem of a crisis of authority in the Muslim world, they forget that this is not just a situation that arose in modernity. What is interesting, however, is that each of the two faiths has significant internal divisions on matters of political theology.

G.G.: What about the division we hear so much about in the news, between Shias and Sunnis? Could you say a bit about that?

S.R.: Shi'a Islam is a religious tradition in which it is precisely the presence of the divine through the imam—the successor to Muhammad in his bloodline— that provides not only the foundations for authority and sovereignty in human communities of belief, but also the path to salvation. The everlasting and indeed ever-revealing countenance of the divine mentioned in the Quran (28:88, for example) is glossed in the tradition as the person of the imam. The imam is not the defender of the Law; he is the Law—he is not the exegete of scripture, he is revelation itself. Through the person of the imam, the transcendent divine, the origin and the true king, is manifest; and believers follow the path to salvation through their devotion and obedience to the imam. In fact, from early on, Islam seems to have held that believers' afterlife depends on their allegiance to their community. In this sense, Shia is a normative political theology, concerned with the relation of political authority and salvation. The comparison with Christ Pantocrator and the person of the emperor in Eastern Orthodox Christianity is rather striking.

G.G.: How does this compare with the Sunni traditions?

S.R.: In contrast to the Sunni, the Shia traditions in Islam have a more absolute notion of the political-theological significance of both sacred history and the beliefs that one holds and the rituals that one practices. Shia political theology speaks of a messianic Twelfth imam, who will come as a redeemer and avenger in the last days, though this theme is routinized and deferred. Sunni traditions tend to be more pragmatic about politics, even though there is a rather atavistic nostalgia about the caliphate as a paradigmatic institution of early Islam—a nostalgia for a golden age that never was. It has always been the normativity of the community and its consensus that is binding which leads to a greater stress on conformity of practice but also leaves space for condemnation of views outside of the consensus as heresy.

But what is essential to remember is that each theological strand and community within Islam claims the true and proper interpretation and practice of the faith for themselves. Therefore, discussing the Shia merely as heretics or those on the margins or outside the "mainstream" community misses the simple point that they consider themselves to be bearers of the original message and the real community of believers who define Islam for themselves and for others.

G.G.: Many people are puzzled at the violent conflicts between Shias and Sunnis. They think that Europe has pretty much gotten past this stage since the Enlightenment, and they wonder why the same thing hasn't happened in Muslim countries.

S.R.: I think we forget that sectarian violence is often forged in the crucible of political conflicts and uncertainty. While there are theological accounts that back the discourses of condemnation in the modern world, the impetus often comes from the scramble for political and economic resources. The basic stability of Europe in opposition to what is happening in Syria and Iraq is the differentiating factor—and even then in times of crisis, as we saw in the former Yugoslavia in the 1990s, sectarian entrepreneurs could be relied upon to manipulate emotions for political gain. There is, of course, the sense that religious feelings even within faiths are strongly held—and this is clear even in Europe and North America. But if one has the rule of law and political stability, that negativity to the other may manifest itself in hate speech but rarely in violence.

G.G.: You've presented what many of our readers may see as a quite moderate and "enlightened" version of Islam. But aren't you ignoring fundamentalist versions of the religion that today are very powerful and directly opposed to liberal values? I'm thinking, for example, of their treatment of women, their demand for Islamic states, and their use of violence to achieve religious goals. Do you think there a need for a reformed Islam that will decisively reject such fundamentalist views?

S.R.: In many ways we live in an age of fundamentalisms—and this is true not just of religious communities. That, coupled with the weakness of traditional scholarly institutions in many Muslim communities, has led to uncertainty about who speaks for the faith and whether anyone can speak definitively for the faith. I have a problem with applying to Islam the standard European account of progress as a process in which conflict with secular thought leads to reform, intellectual enlightenment, and finally the redefinition of faith in terms of beliefs divorced from any communal expression.

What I would argue for is not necessarily reform—I have serious reservations about most reformist agendas as well as forms of "neo-traditionalism"— but rather for a more open debate about the simple acts of reading texts in multiple ways. We need to understand how we might read traditional texts in ways that make sense of our faith for the contexts in which we now live. This is not radical reform, but it is an attempt to keep the dialogue within traditions alive and dynamic across space and time. It is a particular strength of Islam that its intellectual traditions of philosophical theology and spirituality emphasize such dialogue.

G.G.: How do you, as a Muslim, respond to the atheistic claim that, in our age of science, there's no rational basis for accepting theism?

S.R.: I reject the atheistic claim, since I don't believe in a God of gaps and I don't think Islamic intellectual traditions pit science against religion. In those traditions, arguments for the existence of God were not based on scientific observations, but rather on the simple intuition that we cannot reduce everything that we can say about ourselves and about our world to the physical. Atheists may not find arguments for the existence of God compelling, but the arguments at least allow believers to fit their faith in God into a rationally coherent framework. This is why reflection on existence to provide a rational case for believing in God has been a critical element of most Muslim theological traditions.

Alongside those strong traditions of rationality, there have also been fideistic tendencies as well as more experiential responses. What are we to make of the cultural artifacts of our religious civilizations, of the art, poetry, music, and expressions of the self, rooted in an enchantment with some ultimate reality that remains intangible and unscientific? The argument from contingency mentioned above is still one that I think gives a rational account that is coherent. But I also recognize that we are not all rational agents who approach our reality in a purely logical way at all times.

FURTHER THOUGHTS: RELIGION AND REVELATION

My interview with Rizvi presents Islam as a concrete alternative to other monotheistic religions. This provides an opportunity to reflect further on Philip Kitcher's diversity argument, which showed how the existence of mutually incompatible religious views challenge the rationality of accepting any specific religion as the truth. It also opens up the question of whether those who see their religion as the unique revelation of God can tolerate those who reject this revelation.

The diversity challenge becomes particularly difficult to defeat once we focus on sibling religions like Judaism, Christianity, and Islam. Rousseau's Savoyard vicar makes the point vividly: "At the Sorbonne, it is as clear as day that the predictions about the Messiah relate to Jesus Christ. Among the Amsterdam rabbis it is just as clear that they do not have the least relation to Jesus. . . . At Constantinople, the Turks state their arguments, but we do not dare state our own. There it is our turn to crawl" (Jean-Jacques Rousseau, *Emile*, translated by Allan Bloom, Basic Books, 1979, 304). Rousseau also emphasizes that we can't adequately judge a religion merely by its doctrines but must also be familiar with the specifics of its practices and social context. It's hard to avoid concluding that an adequate assessment of Islam (or of other comparably developed religions) would require an inside knowledge of both its teachings and its way of life that hardly any believer in a rival religion could ever achieve.

Suppose, nonetheless, that we have somehow decisively refuted all rivals and are fully convinced that our religion is the one true faith. We then face the question of how to deal with views on a subject of supreme importance (eternal salvation) that we are entirely certain are false. To what extent should we tolerate religious error? In our discussion, Rizvi emphasizes that there are a variety of Muslim responses to this question, some rigorist to the point of requiring violence to suppress unbelief, others supporting various forms of tolerance. Among Jews and Christians, the strongest forms of intolerance nowadays are marginal, whereas they are significant although by no means universal in Islam. The difference seems to be that in most Muslim societies no movement parallel to the Enlightenment has established religious tolerance as a fundamental principle.

But Enlightenment tolerance primarily derives from a weakening of faith in revealed religion. Its major proponents may, like Voltaire, profess a theistic natural religion, but they agree that there was no basis for privileging any purportedly revealed religion as the truth everyone should accept. In the wake of the seventeenth-century wars of religion, those devoted to a particular Christian sect typically accepted religious tolerance of other sects as the price for tolerance of their own. This was a sensible bargain in a world of religious warfare, but it implied (contrary to the ethos of early Christian martyrs) that the truth was not worth dying for and (contrary to the spirit of the Crusades) that it is not worth killing for. An entrenched policy of toleration eventually led to secular states in which religions existed only as private practices, with none endorsed by the state or society as a whole.

This privatization of religion transforms the authority of religious institutions, which no longer have any political power to impose their beliefs and practices on individuals. Bishops and pastors may claim an objective authority, ordained by God, over the members of their congregations. But in fact they have no more authority than their adherents choose to give them. The principle of religious toleration in a secular state acknowledges the absolute right of an individual's conscience in religious matters. Most churches acknowledge this right, even an authoritarian hierarchical organization like the Catholic Church, which insists that no one may "be prevented from acting according to his conscience, especially in religious matters", according to a decree of the Second Vatican Council. The official Catholic view still maintains that a conscience that rejects the hierarchy's formal teaching is "objectively" in error. But it acknowledges that subjectively individuals not only may but also should act on their sincere beliefs. Even sects that deny the right of members to leave have no legal basis for forcing them to stay.

This is not to deny the obvious fact that religious groups— like American fundamentalists—are politically active and even successful in a secular society. But even the most doctrinally driven groups need to make their public cases in primarily secular terms. So, for example, conservative Catholics argue that abortion is murder and that homosexual behavior is contrary to a "natural law" derivable from rational argument. Similarly, in public debates about evolution, evangelical Christians rely on philosophical arguments for intelligent design rather than biblical texts about divine creation. To the extent that these religiously neutral arguments fail to convince, the political agendas of churches become increasingly ineffective. For example, the reversal on gay marriage in the United States was partly due to the intellectual collapse (even among Catholics) of increasingly convoluted natural-law arguments against homosexual behavior. On the other hand, the continuing appeal of arguments based on the humanity of the fetus helps keep the anti-abortion cause alive.

The United States remains distinctive among North Atlantic nations in its citizens' sympathy for the idea that their democracy is rooted in a belief in God. The Declaration of Independence cites "the laws of nature and of nature's God" as the support for our rights, and a majority of Americans remain comfortable with mottos such as "In God We Trust" on coins and "one nation, under God" in the Pledge of Allegiance (both introduced in the mid-twentieth century to differentiate our system from that of "godless communism"). Such things set us apart from the more secular democracies of Western Europe. But they at best express a quasi-official commitment to theistic natural religion, not to any revealed religion. Although most of the founders of the American republic had some connection to (mostly Protestant) Christianity, there was little need for appeals to revelation to ground their political philosophy. The deism so influential among educated Americans of the time was a sufficient foundation. And, of course, the Constitutional separation of church and state eliminated any notion of an official state religion.

Nevertheless, according to Pew Research data, about 70 percent of Americans identify as Christians, and among members of Congress in 2015, the percentage was 92 percent. It may be that the doctrinal beliefs of many self-declared Christians amount to little more than a deistic natural religion. But in the United States, in contrast to western European democracies, a politician who is not a Christian (or a Jew) is likely to be at a considerable disadvantage. The prospects for self-declared atheists or even agnostics are, of course, much dimmer.

Despite the important residual role of Christianity, the United States is not a major exception to the diluting effect that Enlightenment thought has had on Western religions. In countries with a large population of Muslims, Islam has a diverse range of roles. Islamic states, such as Iran and Saudi Arabia, accept Islamic law as the political foundation of their nations; others, such as Egypt and Iraq, are not founded on Islamic law but privilege Islam as the official state religion; still others remain officially neutral regarding the status of Islam (like Indonesia) or officially secular (like Turkey), although they have large Muslim populations and Islam plays an important role in their political life. But overall, the doctrines of revealed religion have a social and political influence in Muslim countries that such doctrines lack in Christian countries. The ideas of Enlightenment secularism have seriously transformed the concrete significance of Christian faith.

9

Hinduism: Divinity Without God

(Jonardon Ganeri)

So far, my interviewees and I have, in line with this book's title, been talking about God—the supremely great person Jews, Christians, and Muslims worship. But although a bit more than 50 percent of the world's people belong to these monotheist religions, close to 40 percent are either Hindus or Buddhists, religions that are not focused on a supreme person. Hindus, for example, often have, as Jonardon Ganeri emphasizes in the following interview, "nontheistic concepts of the divine".

It may seem that such talk makes no sense: doesn't "the divine" mean "God" and isn't a concept of God a theistic concept? But although divinity must be in some sense the ultimate reality, it doesn't follow that such reality must be personal. God, as understood by Jews, Christians, and Muslims is a person, but there is room for an ultimate reality other than God; for, in other words, a nontheistic divinity. Many Hindus do worship various gods, such as Vishnu, Shiva, and the Goddess (as well as a multitude of lesser deities), who appear as vivid characters in engaging narratives. But the divinity (ultimate reality) that is the primary focus of Hinduism is typically not a person.

Further, Hindu thought offers several quite different conceptions of nontheistic divinity. For example, the seminal Hindu religious text known as the Veda is sometimes taken not as a group of books that we can read but as the eternal structure defining the meaning of the world. Divinity is also conceived as the essential reality underlying the flux of appearances that occupy ordinary human life, or as the inward subjectivity of every person regarded not as an individual but as a universal consciousness identical for everyone.

This plurality of conceptions of the divine is just one example of the diversity that Hindu religion embraces, although it is especially important. In fact, the religion contains so many different and even conflicting elements that there are scholarly disputes about whether we should speak of Hinduisms rather than Hinduism. The singular term originated in eighteenth- and nineteenth-century efforts of Westerners to understand diverse local Indian practices on the model of the major monotheistic religions, although the term has become common among Hindus themselves. Nonetheless, it is difficult to specify a core of essential beliefs and practices that would characterize all Hindus. It is probably better to think of the religion in terms of family resemblances, with different Hindu communities characterized by different selections from a large set of sacred texts, gods, ideas of divinity, rituals, spiritual exercises, and so on.

This diversity makes Hinduism a fruitful source for those

dissatisfied with the limited range of views that dominate Western thinking about religion. There are not only alternative conceptions of divinity but also other ways of thinking about the afterlife (reincarnation, loss of individual self in an ultimate reality), methods of meditation more highly developed than those of Western religions, and even distinctive—and rigorously formulated—philosophical systems that arose independently of ancient Greek thought. My interview with Ganeri, who is a philosopher and a leading scholar of Hindu thought, touches on these and other resources in Hindu religion.

INTERVIEW WITH JONARDON GANERI[*]

Gary Gutting: How might looking at Hinduism alter philosophical approaches to religion that take Christianity as their primary example?

Jonardon Ganeri: Taking Christianity as the exemplar of religion skews philosophical discussion towards attempts to solve, resolve, or dissolve difficult philosophical puzzles inherent in monotheism: problems about God's powers, goodness, and knowledge; attempts to provide rational arguments for God's existence; the problem of evil; and so on. Hindu philosophers have traditionally been far more interested in a quite different array of problems, especially questions about the nature of religious knowledge and religious language, initially

---

[*] This interview was originally published as "What Would Krishna Do? Or Shiva? Or Vishnu?" *The Stone* (blog), *New York Times*, August 3, 2014.

arising from their concerns with the Veda as a sacred eternal text and as a source of ritual and moral law.

G.G.: Does this mean that Hinduism is a religion without God?

J.G.: Many Hindus believe in God, but not all in the same god: For some it is Vishnu, for others Shiva, for others again it is rather the Goddess. Some of the more important Hindu philosophers are atheists, arguing that no sacred religious text such as the Veda could be the word of God, since authorship, even divine authorship, implies the logical possibility of error. Whether believed in or not, a personal god does not figure prominently as the source of the idea of the divine, and instead nontheistic concepts of the divine prevail.

G.G.: What do you mean by "nontheistic" concepts of the divine?

J.G.: One such concept sees the text of the Veda as itself divine. Its language, on this view, has a structure that is prior to and isomorphic with the structure of the world and its grammar is complete (although parts may have been lost over the centuries). The divinity of the text inverts the order of priority between text and author: Now, at best, assignment of authorship is a cataloguing device not the identification of origin. Recitation of the text is itself a religious act.

Another Hindu conception of the divine is that

it is the essential reality in comparison to which all else is only concealing appearance. This is the concept one finds in the Upanishads. Philosophically the most important claim the Upanishads make is that the essence of each person is also the essence of all things; the human self and *brahman* (the essential reality) are the same.

This identity claim leads to a third conception of the divine: that inwardness or interiority or subjectivity is itself a kind of divinity. On this view, religious practice is contemplative, taking time to turn one's gaze inwards to find one's real self; but—and this point is often missed—there is something strongly anti-individualistic in this practice of inwardness, since the deep self one discovers is the same self for all.

G.G.: Could you say something about the Hindu view of life after death? In particular, are Hindu philosophers able to make sense of the notion of reincarnation?

J.G.: Every religion has something to say about death and the afterlife, and hence engages with philosophical questions about the metaphysics of the self. While Christian philosophy of self tends to be limited to a single conception of self as immortal soul, Hindu philosophers have experimented with an astonishing range of accounts of self, some of which are at the cutting edge in contemporary philosophy of mind.

G.G.: Could you give an example?

J.G.: The self as an immaterial, immortal soul is consistent with the Hindu idea of survival through reincarnation. But some Hindu philosophers have concluded that mind and the mental must be embodied. If so, reincarnation requires that mental states must be able to be "multiply realized" in different physical states. This led to the idea, much later popular among analytic philosophers of mind, that the mental is a set of functions that operate through the body. Such an approach supports the idea that there is a place for the self within nature, that a self—even one that exists over time in different bodies—need be not a supernatural phenomenon.

G.G.: What sort of ethical guidance does Hinduism provide?

J.G.: One of the most important texts in the religious life of many Hindus is the *Bhagavad-gītā*, the Song of the Lord. The Gītā is deeply philosophical, addressing in poetic, inspirational language a fundamental conundrum of human existence: what to do when one is pulled in different directions by different sorts of obligation, how to make hard choices. The hard choice faced by the protagonist Arjuna is whether to go to war against members of his own family, in violation of a universal duty not to kill; or to abstain, letting a wrong go unrighted and breaking a duty that is uniquely his. Lord Krishna counsels Arjuna with the philosophical advice that the moral motivation for action should never consist in expected outcomes, that one should act but not base one's path of action on one's wants or needs.

G.G.: This sounds rather like the Kantian view that morality means doing what's right regardless of the consequences.

J.G.: There are ongoing debates about what sort of moral philosophy Krishna is proposing—Amartya Sen has claimed that he's a quasi-Kantian but others disagree. More important than this scholarly debate, though, is what the text tells us about how to live: that living is hard, and doing the right thing is difficult; that leading a moral life is at best an enigmatic and ambiguous project. No escape route from moral conflict by imitating the actions of a morally perfect individual is on offer here. Krishna, unlike Christ, the Buddha, or Muhammad is not portrayed as morally perfect, and indeed the philosopher Bimal Matilal very aptly describes him as the "devious divinity". We can but try our best in treacherous circumstances.

G.G.: How does the notion of "karma" fit into the picture?

J.G.: Let me be clear. The idea of karma is that every human action has consequences, but it is not at all the claim that every human action is itself a consequence. So the idea of karma does not imply a fatalistic outlook on life, according to which one's past deeds predeter-

mine all one's actions. The essence of the theory is simply that one's life will be better if one acts in ways that
are ethical, and it will be worse if one acts in ways that
are unethical.

A claim like that can be justified in many different
ways. Buddhism, for example, tends to give it a strictly
causal interpretation (bad actions make bad things happen). But I think that within Hinduism, karma is more
like what Kant called a postulate of practical reason,
something one does well to believe in and act according
to (for Kant, belief in God was a practical postulate of
this sort).

G.G.: How does Hinduism regard other religions (for
example, as teaching falsehoods, as worthy alternative
ways, as partial insights into its fuller truth)?

J.G.: The essence of Hinduism is that it has no essence.
What defines Hinduism and sets it apart from other
major religions is its polycentricity, its admission of
multiple centers of belief and practice, with a consequent absence of any single structure of theological
or liturgical power. Unlike Christianity, Buddhism,
or Islam, there is no one single canonical text—the
Bible, the Dialogues of the Buddha, the Quran—that
serves as a fundamental axis of hermeneutical or doctrinal endeavor, recording the words of a foundational
religious teacher. (The Veda is only the earliest in a
diverse corpus of Hindu texts.) Hinduism is a banyan
tree, in the shade of whose canopy, supported by not

one but many trunks, a great diversity of thought and action is sustained.

G.G.: Would Hinduism require rejecting the existence of the God worshipped by Christians, Jews, or Muslims?

J.G.: No, it wouldn't. To the extent that Hindus worship one god, they tend to be henotheists, that is, worshiping their god but not denying the existence of others ("every individual worships some god", not "some god is worshipped by every individual"). The henotheistic attitude can accept the worship of the Abrahamic God as another practice of the same kind as the worship of Vishnu or Shiva (and Vaishnavism and Shaivism are practically different religions under the catchall rubric "Hinduism").

Without a center, there can be no periphery either, and so Hinduism's approach to other religions tends to be incorporationist. In practice this can imply a disrespect for the otherness of non-Hindu religious traditions, and in particular of their ability to challenge or call into question Hindu beliefs and practices. The positive side is that there is in Hinduism a long heritage of tolerance of dissent and difference.

One explanation of this tolerance of difference is that religious texts are often not viewed as making truth claims, which might then easily contradict one another. Instead, they are seen as devices through which one achieves self-transformation. Reading a religious text, taking it to heart, appreciating it, is a transformative experience, and in the transformed state one might well become aware that the claims of the text would, were they taken literally, be false. So religious texts are seen in Hinduism as "Trojan texts" (like the Trojan horse, but breaking through mental walls in disguise). Such texts enter the mind of the reader and help constitute the self.

The Hindu attitude to the Bible or the Quran is the same, meaning that the sorts of disagreements that arise from literalist readings of the texts tend not to arise.

G.G.: What ultimate good does Hinduism promise those who follow it, and what is the path to attaining this good?

J.G.: The claim is that there are three pathways, of equal merit, leading in their own way to liberation. Hindu philosophers have employed a good deal of logical skill in their definitions of liberation. To cut a long story short, for some it is a state defined as the endless but not beginingless absence of pain; others characterize it as a state of bliss. The three pathways are the path of knowledge, the path of religious performance, and the path of devotion. The path of knowledge requires philosophical reflection, that of religious performances various rituals and good deeds, and that of devotion worship and service, often of a particular deity such as Krishna.

G.G.: Could you say a bit more about the path of knowledge and its relation to philosophy?

J.G.: Knowledge can liberate because epistemic error is the primary source of anguish, and knowledge is an antidote to error. I might err, for example, if I believe that I only need to satisfy my current desires in order to be happy. The antidote is the knowledge that the satisfaction of one desire serves only to generate another.

According to the Nyāya philosopher Vātsyāyana, this is why philosophy is important. Doing philosophy is the way we cultivate our epistemic skills, learning to tell sound doxastic practices from bogus ones, and the cultivation of epistemic skills is what stops the merry-go-round between cognitive error and mental distress. So it isn't that philosophy and religion are not distinct, but that there is a meta-theory about their relationship.

G.G.: The liberation you've described seems to be a matter of escaping from the cares of this world. Doesn't this lead to a lack of interest in social and political action to make this world better?

J.G.: The great narrative texts of Hinduism are the two epics, the *Mahābhārata* and the *Rāmāyaṇa*. These epics are drawn on as resources in thinking about ethical conduct, forms of just society, and the possibility of various kinds of political and social agency. They are vast polycentric texts, and are read as such by Hindus. One of the important virtues of these epics is that they give voice to a range of participants within Hinduism that tend to go unheard: women, the disenfranchised, the outsider, the migrant. They provide these groups with important models for social and political intervention. That's one reason they have always been very popular works within the Hindu diaspora.

The mirror image of the idea that liberation consists in the absence of distress is that a free society consists in the absence of injustice; thus the removal of injustice, rather than the creation of a perfect or ideal society, is the target of political action. Just as the absence of distress is a minimal condition compatible with many different kinds of human well-being (we are back to the theme of polycentricism), so the absence of injustice is compatible with many different types of well-ordered communities or societies.

G.G.: How do you respond to the charge that Hinduism has supported the injustices of the caste system in India?

J.G.: I think it is important to see that Hinduism contains *within itself* the philosophical resources to sustain an internal critique of reprehensible and unjust social practices that have sometimes emerged in Hindu societies. For example, Hindu social reformers have drawn on the Upanishadic idea that all selves are equal, and one with *brahman* to challenge the system of caste. More generally, Manu's Code of Law, which is often seen as laying down the foundations for caste, is no more canonical than any other of the great diversity and plurality of Hindu texts that have social implications, some composed by non-Brahman and some featuring strong women characters. There are thus forms of rational self-criticism that the diverse riches of Hindu philosophy enable, and an individual's social identity as a Hindu is something to be actively fashioned from a plurality of traditional materials rather than merely inherited.

FURTHER THOUGHTS:
A DIFFERENT PICTURE OF RELIGION

Hinduism is perhaps most valuable to our thinking about religion as a counterexample to a standard Western picture of how religions develop. That picture begins with the widely used distinction between a traditional and a modern society. The hallmark of a traditional society is that its members see no meaningful alternatives to its core beliefs and practices. If women care for children and men hunt for food or if the eldest son must marry and produce heirs and the youngest son must enter a monastery, then those affected by this rule cannot envisage acting against it. They may know of other peoples who behave differently, but they regard that as a sign of their essentially alien character. There is no meaningful alternative to living according to the role society assigns. In a modern society, almost any core belief or practice is open to challenge. Such things as the king's powers, women's place, and children's duties are subject to scrutiny, criticism, and revision.

Religion is typically part of the core of a traditional society. Denial of the gods or disrespect for sacred rituals can only be signs of madness. Thinking and living in terms the community's religion is part of each individual's identity. With the transition into modernity, people start to see their religious beliefs and practices as open to question. As a result, a society may well splinter into many subgroups with diverse beliefs and practices. Although religion does not disappear, it becomes a matter of individual preference and no longer defines what it means to be a member of the community.

The history of Christianity from the Middle Ages to the present is typically read as an illustration of the fate of religion in this sort of move from a traditional to modern society. Once the Reformation broke the medieval unity of faith, the door was open to the Enlightenment critiques that challenged its religious authority. This, combined with various social and economic changes, eliminated religious faith as a defining feature of the Western way of life.

Hinduism, however, does not fit this picture. It is the majority religion of India, comprising 80 percent of the population (for a total of about 1 billion adherents). Although modernity now has a strong influence, there are hundreds of millions of Indians who, in the traditional manner, see Hindu religion as essential to their identity. Contrary to the Christian model this commitment persists in spite of (or, more likely, because of) the enormous diversity of Hindu belief and practice. Here diversity seems to sustain the religious commitment of a traditional society.

Why this difference? The major monotheistic religions claim that the person in charge of the universe has intervened in our history to tell us, in considerable detail, what we need to believe and how we must behave if we are to attain the heavenly salvation he offers us. Hinduism is far less specific, offering instead a variety of ideas, stories, and practices, often inconsistent with one another but still authentically Hindu. Specific groups follow their own paths while respecting those who go other ways. We might say that Judaism, Christianity, and Islam are religions of *knowledge*, whereas Hinduism is a religion of *understanding*.

Knowledge is a matter of seeing things just as they are. It implies a reality that can be fixed in our minds as at least a practical certainty. What we cannot know we can often understand in a variety of ways that may even be inconsistent with one another. Each catches some aspect of its object, even though it falls short of a perfect grasp. Hinduism readily admits that it lacks knowledge of divinity (ultimate reality) and therefore welcomes alternative modes of understanding. This is why it has no problem accepting a variety of gods, theologies, and devotions. It tells Christians that they can be Hindus and still worship Christ. But the price of accepting this invitation is giving up the exclusive claims of Christianity. Worship of Christ rather than Krishna, for example, can only be a matter of personal preference.

Monotheists reject this sort of tolerance because they see their competing revelations as expressions of infallible divine knowledge. This, however, ignores the unbridgeable gap between the divine and the human. Even if we know that our scriptures contain God's knowledge, there is no basis for thinking that this knowledge can be adequately fixed in our minds. Monotheists acknowledge this by emphasizing the "mysteries" of their faith, but this emphasis is most often used as a way of deflecting objections to doctrines rather than as grounds for recognizing alternatives to them. Given the conviction that

God has spoken directly to us, it is hard to give up the idea that we have his truth. This idea is reinforced by the belief that there is a chain extending from those (Moses, the Apostles, Muhammad) who received the original revelation to current religious authorities. The interest in preserving this authority typically masks the teaching on the incomprehensibility of God's truth.

At the same time, however, the monotheist insistence on exclusive truth inevitably leads to intractable disagreements about what that truth is. The ship of dogma is always buffeted by the winds of heresy. In the case of Christianity, this eventually led to a splintering into many rival religions, which, as we've noted, led to a general undermining of the social role of religion. The result has been a steady trend toward the sort of diversity characteristic of Hinduism, but in a way that lodged Christian churches in the private sphere, without the social authority of a traditional religion.

A philosophy of religion that takes Hinduism seriously need not turn away from the problematics corresponding to the distinctive features of monotheist religions. But it will have to put these religions in a wider context, where it becomes clear that some of their concerns reflect not the essential logic of religious thought and experience but rather the peculiarities of their contingent historical situation.

10

BUDDHISM: RELIGION WITHOUT DIVINITY

(JAY GARFIELD)

We've seen how Hinduism expands our conception of what a religion might be, and how this might challenge elements of Abrahamic religions. In my interview with Jay Garfield, we turn to Buddhism, the other great religion of East Asia, which grew out of Hinduism and seems to take us even further from the monotheist personal god. In fact, Buddhism suggests the possibility of a thoroughly naturalistic religion that entirely excludes not just a divine person but also any supernatural divinity.

Instead of adding divinity to the natural world, Buddhism offers a reinterpretation of what that world is. According to commonsense thinking, the world consists primarily of relatively stable things (mountains, plants, animals, people) that are capable of changing, but in most cases, preserve their identities through these changes. This is the view enshrined not only in commonsense and everyday speech but also in Aristotle's metaphysics (where the stable things are called substances). It is even present in the physics of Newton, which merely adds that macroscopic substances are in fact aggregates of microscopic substances (e.g., molecules or atoms).

Buddhism, however, understands our world not as one in which identities and properties are relatively stable but as one in which, as Garfield puts it, "all phenomena are impermanent and constantly changing". There are no independent, self-identical entities. Moreover, this fundamental truth about the world is not accepted on faith, as the revelation of a divinity, but as a human discovery. The Buddha who proclaimed this truth was not God's messenger. He had discovered the truth through his own meditation, and tried to help others make the same discovery. In Buddhism, "awakening" is not received from a god but achieved by humans themselves. The same is true of the other fundamental Buddhist truths, found, as Garfield explains, in the "three refuges" and the "four noble truths".

INTERVIEW WITH JAY GARFIELD[*]

Gary Gutting: Philosophy of religion typically focuses on questions and disputes about the ideas and doctrines of monotheistic religions, with Christianity the primary model. How does the discussion change if we add Buddhism, which is neither monotheistic nor polytheistic, as a primary model of a religion?

Jay Garfield: What gets called "philosophy of religion" in most philosophy departments and journals is really

---

* This interview was originally published as "What Does Buddhism Require?" in *The Stone* (blog), *New York Times*, April 27, 2014.

philosophy of Abrahamic religion: basically, Judaism, Christianity, and Islam. Most of the questions addressed in those discussions are simply irrelevant to most of the world's other religious traditions. Philosophers look at other religious traditions with the presumption that they are more or less the same, at least in outline, as the Abrahamic religions, and even fight about whether other traditions count as religions at all based upon their sharing certain features of the Abrahamic religions. That is a serious ethnocentrism that can really blind us to important phenomena. For instance, I recently moderated a discussion in Singapore with A. C. Grayling, who claimed that Buddhism is not a religion because Buddhists don't believe in a supreme being. This simply ignores the fact that many religions are not theistic in this sense. Chess is a game, despite the fact that it is not played with a ball, after all.

Now, when we address Buddhism, we must be very careful. The Buddhist world is vast, and Buddhism has been around in various forms for two and a half millennia. There are many forms of Buddhist practice and culture, many Buddhist communities of belief and practice, and significant doctrinal differences among Buddhist schools. So generalization can be dangerous. Just as we need to be careful about lumping Unitarians and Catholics together when we ask whether Christians accept the transubstantiation of the host, we must be careful about lumping together, for instance, Theravada monks in Sri Lanka with lay Zen practitioners in San Francisco. And there is no central doctrinal authority or organization that covers all of the Buddhist world.

Still, there are some widely shared features of Buddhism that would make a philosophy of religion that took it seriously look quite different. First, since Buddhism is an atheistic religion, it doesn't raise questions about the existence of God that so dominate the philosophy of Abrahamic religions, let alone questions about the attributes of the deity. Buddhists do worry about awakening (Buddhahood). How hard is it to achieve? What is it like? Is a Buddha aware of her surroundings, or do they disappear as illusory? Buddhists worry about the relation between ordinary reality, or conventional truth, and ultimate reality. Are they the same or different? Is the world fundamentally illusory, or is it real? They worry about hermeneutical questions concerning the intent of apparently conflicting canonical scriptures, and how to resolve them. They ask about the nature of the person, and its relationship to more fundamental psychophysical processes. Stuff like that. The philosophy of religion looks different if these are taken to be some of its fundamental questions.

G.G.: Given these widely shared features, would you venture to say what, overall, it is to be a Buddhist?

J.G.: To be a Buddhist is to take refuge in the three Buddhist refuge objects (often called "the three jewels"): the Buddha, Dharma, and Sangha. To take refuge is to see human existence as fundamentally unsatisfactory and to see the three jewels as the only solution to this predicament.

The first refuge object is the Buddha: the fact that at least one person—the historical Buddha Siddhartha Gautama—has achieved awakening and release from suffering. This provides hope in one's own future awakening, hope that through practice one can achieve a satisfactory existence. The second refuge is Dharma, or Buddhist doctrine. The third is the Sangha, or spiritual community, conceived sometimes as the community of other practitioners, sometimes as the community of monks and nuns, sometimes as the community of awakened beings. The project of full awakening is a collective, not an individual, venture.

G.G.: The first and the third refuges seem to correspond to a way of life, justified simply by its results in relieving suffering. What's involved in the second refuge, the doctrines?

J.G.: The foundation of doctrine in all Buddhist schools is the so-called four noble truths, explained by Siddhartha in his first talk after gaining awakening. The first is that life is fundamentally unsatisfactory, permeated by suffering of various types, including pain, aging and death, and the inability to control one's own destiny. The second is that this suffering is caused by attraction and aversion—attraction to things one can't have, and aversion to things one can't avoid, and that this attraction and aversion is in turn caused by primal confusion about the fundamental nature of reality and a consequent egocentric orientation to the world. The third is that if one extirpates these causes by eliminating attraction and aversion through metaphysical insight, one can eliminate suffering. The fourth is the specification of a set of domains and concerns—the eightfold path—attention to which can accomplish that.

G.G.: It seems then that the Buddhist way of life is based on, first, the plausible claim that suffering makes life unsatisfactory and, second, on a psychological account—again plausible—of the causes of suffering. But what's the "metaphysical insight", the truth about reality, that shows the way to eliminating suffering?

J.G.: Buddhist doctrine regarding the nature of reality generally focuses on three principal characteristics of things. The first idea is that all phenomena are impermanent and constantly changing, despite the fact that we engage with them as though they are permanent; the second is that they are interdependent, although we engage with them as though they are independent; the third is that they are without any intrinsic identity, although we treat ourselves and other objects as though they have intrinsic identities.

Now, many Buddhists and Buddhist schools are committed to much more extensive and detailed metaphysical doctrines, including doctrines about the fundamental constituents of reality, or dharmas, often conceived as momentary instances of properties, or about the nature of consciousness, or about cosmology. Buddhist schools and traditions vary widely in these respects. And of course there are vast differences between what lay Buddhists and what scholars understand about Buddhist doctrine. In Buddhism, as in Christianity, for many laypeople the religion is about daily rituals and practices, and doctrine is left to scholars and clerics. And ideas that are complex metaphors to the erudite are literal for the laity.

G.G.: You haven't mentioned what, to many outsiders, might seem the most striking Buddhist doctrine: reincarnation.

J.G.: I would, first, drop the term "reincarnation", which has a more natural home in a Hindu context, in favor of "rebirth", which makes more sense in a Buddhist context. That is because we must understand this doctrine in relation to the central doctrine in all Buddhist schools: that there is no self or soul. So there is nothing that takes on new bodies as does the soul in the Hindu traditions from which Buddhism arose and against which it reacted. Indeed, given the radical Buddhist notion of momentary impermanence, we can say without exaggeration that one is reborn every moment. Buddhism is an Indian tradition, and rebirth across biological lives is taken for granted in most classical Indian philosophical and religious traditions. Buddhism takes that over, and it is taken for granted in many Buddhist traditions that the same kinds of causal continuity that obtain among subsequent stages within a life obtain between stages of our current biological lives and those of past and future biological lives. Many Buddhists would even take this to be an essential commitment of the religious tradition. But in some Buddhist traditions, especially those of East Asia, this view plays no role at all, and many Western Buddhists reject it altogether.

G.G.: How do Buddhists think of other religions? On the one hand, there seems to be a tolerance and even an appreciation for a diversity of views. On the other hand, there is a strong history of missionary activity, aimed at conversion.

J.G.: Exactly right. And again, we must be careful about taking the Abrahamic traditions as a default framework in which to pose this question. The Abrahamic religions all prohibit syncretism, or the melding of beliefs from different creeds, but this is not a common feature of world religious traditions. Many Buddhists are syncretic to some degree. In Japan it is common to practice both Buddhism and Shinto; in Nepal many adopt Buddhist and Hindu practices; in China, Daoism, Confuciansim, and Buddhism blend happily. And Thomas Merton was a Catholic priest and a Buddhist practitioner.

But Buddhism has always been missionary. Buddhists have always thought that their doctrine and practices can help to alleviate suffering and so have urged others to accept them. Sometimes acceptance of Buddhist practices requires one to rethink other religious commitments; sometimes the two can be integrated. Sometimes there is creative tension.

G.G.: I can see Buddhist missionaries making an attractive case for their practices of meditation and their ethics of compassion. But the doctrine of rebirth—which, if true, would make a huge difference in how we view human existence—seems very implausible. How do Buddhists defend this doctrine?

J.G.: Once again, there is diversity here. Some Buddhists don't defend the doctrine at all, either because they take it to be the obvious default position, as it is in some cultures, particularly in South Asia, or because it is not important or taken seriously, as in some East Asian or Western traditions. But others do defend it. One popular approach is an empirical argument: to wit, that some people have clear memories of past lives or make clear and accurate predictions about their next lives. One sees this primarily in the Tibetan tradition in which there is a widespread practice of identifying rebirths and of rebirth lineages for high lamas, such as the Dalai Lama.

G.G.: I suspect that people not already culturally disposed to accept rebirth aren't likely to find such evidence convincing.

J.G.: Another approach is that of the Indian philosopher Dharmakirti, who argues for the necessity of believing in rebirth, though not directly for its reality. Dharmakirti argues that given the stupendous difficulty of achieving full awakening, the cultivation of a genuine aspiration to achieve awakening, which is essential to Mahayana Buddhist practice, requires one to believe in future lives; otherwise, one could not have the confidence in the possibility of success necessary to genuine resolution. This is worth comparing to Kant's argument that one must believe in free will in order to act and in order to treat oneself and others as moral agents, which nonetheless is not a direct argument for the freedom of the will, only for the necessity of the belief for moral life.

G.G.: Kant's argument has received a lot of criticism from philosophers. Do you think Dharmakirti's works?

J.G.: No, I have argued elsewhere that this is a bad argument for its intended conclusion. It confuses a commitment to the existence of future lives with a commitment to the existence of one's own future life, and a commitment to the attainment of awakening with a commitment to one's own awakening. But I do think it's a good argument for an important conclusion in the neighborhood. For the aspiration for awakening—for a complete, liberating understanding of the nature of reality and of human life—need not, and should not, for a Mahayana Buddhist, be personalized. Just as a stonemason building the ground floor of a medieval cathedral might aspire to its completion even if he knows that he will not personally be around to be involved in its completion, a practitioner who aspires that awakening will be achieved need not believe that she will be around to see it, but only hope that her own conduct and practice will facilitate that.

So, this suggests one way for a Buddhist not taken with the idea of personal rebirth across biological lives to take that doctrine as a useful metaphor: treat the past reflectively and with gratitude and responsibility, and with an awareness that much of our present life is conditioned by our collective past; take the future seriously as something we have the responsibility to construct, just as much as if we would be there personally. This makes sense of the ideas, for instance, of intergenerational justice, or of collective contemporary responsibility for harms inflicted in the past, as well as our current personal responsibility to future generations.

As Buddhism takes root in the West and as Asian Buddhist traditions engage with modernity, we will see how doctrines such as this persist, fade, or are adapted. One thing we can see from the long and multicultural history of Buddhism is that it has always deeply affected the cultures into which it has moved, and has always been transformed in important ways by those cultures.

G.G.: Won't the fundamental denial of a self be hard to maintain in the face of the modern emphasis on individuality?

J.G.: I don't think so. For one thing, note that the view that there is no substantial self has a history in the West as well, in the thought of Hume, and of Nietzsche. For another, note that many contemporary cognitive scientists and philosophers have either rejected the view that there is such a self, or have defended some variety of a minimalist conception of the self. So the doctrine isn't as secure in the non-Buddhist world as one might think. And this may be a good thing, not only for metaphysical reasons. A strong sense of self—of one's own substantial reality, uniqueness, and independence of others—may not be psychologically or morally healthy. It can lead to egoism, to narcissism, and to a lack of care for others. So the modern emphasis on individuality you mention might not be such a good thing. We might all be better off if we each took ourselves less seriously as selves. That may be one of the most important Buddhist critiques of modernity and contributions to postmodernity.

More positively, the Buddhist tradition encourages us to see ourselves as impermanent, interdependent individuals, linked to one another and to our world through shared commitments to achieving an understanding of our lives and a reduction of suffering. It encourages us to rethink egoism and to consider an orientation to the world characterized by care and joint responsibility. That can't be a bad thing.

FURTHER THOUGHTS: A RELIGION FOR ATHEISTS?

Given this understanding of Buddhism, it might seem that an atheist who thinks there is nothing beyond the natural world could be a Buddhist. This is the view that Sam Harris, one of the most prominent New Atheists, develops in his book *Waking Up: A Guide to Spirituality Without Religion* (Simon & Schuster, 2014). He cites Buddhist meditation to justify what he sees as a life-transforming insight into the unreality of our ordinary ways of thinking. In particular, meditation reveals that the self does not exist: "the feeling that we call 'I' is an illusion". Harris maintains that this insight has central ethical significance. It shows how it is "possible to find lasting fulfillment despite the inevitability of change" (17).

We might think that such claims go beyond anything that a tough-minded atheist could accept. If there's nothing beyond the natural world, isn't empirical science the sole arbiter of what there is? And isn't an appeal to some sort of subjective "mystical experience" just more religious mumbo-jumbo?

Harris acknowledges that many Buddhists fall into super-stitious and cultish beliefs in such things as gods and magical powers. But, he insists, the central Buddhist claim of fulfill-ment by escaping from the illusion of the self does not rest on an irrational faith. It is something that any of us can see for ourselves by attentive introspection. In fact, Harris puts the nonexistence of the self on a par with scientific observa-tion. Unlike most religious believers, Buddhists do not see the truths of meditation as a divine revelation accepted on faith. Rather, the truths follow from "empirical instructions: If you do X, you will experience Y" (30). Therefore, an empirically minded atheist could undertake training in Buddhist medita-tion (as Harris has) and accept in good conscience the deliv-erances of such meditation.

But how can Harris put the purely subjective process of

introspective meditation on a par with the objectivity of scientific observation? To this Harris, who has a PhD in neuroscience, has a very interesting response. He begins by insisting that, although "consciousness is 'subjective'", this is "not in the pejorative sense of being unscientific, biased, or *merely* personal". It is, of course, "intrinsically first-person, experiential, and qualitative", but as such it is irreducible to any unconscious processes: "the only thing in this universe that suggests the reality of consciousness is consciousness itself." Because of this, he argues, "the primary approach to understanding consciousness in neuroscience entails correlating changes in its contents with changes in the brain. But no matter how reliable these correlations become, they won't allow us to drop the first-person side of the equation. The experiential character of consciousness is part of the very reality we are studying." From this he concludes that "science needs to be extended to include a disciplined approach to introspection" ("Sam Harris's Vanishing Self," *The Stone* [blog], *New York Times,* September 7, 2014). Buddhist meditation, Harris maintains, is just such a disciplined approach.

Many atheists will think that by accepting consciousness as an irreducibly subjective reality, Harris has abandoned the scientific standpoint that they see as fundamental to their rejection of religion. Science, they no doubt think, has shown that everything that exists is material, and what is material is open to objective observation. Consciousness is certainly real. But, they will say, in the end its reality consists entirely of material processes in the brain, and everything about it can be known by careful neurological study of the brain.

This atheistic response raises a forbidding thicket of philosophical and scientific questions—constituting the mind-body problem—that we would be foolish to enter here. But we do need to note a crucial distinction between a naturalist and a materialist viewpoint. Naturalism holds that there are no realities except those accessible to ordinary human experience and the scientific knowledge based on that experience. "Ordinary experience" includes both sense perception and our introspective awareness of our minds. It rejects the supernatural beings (God, immortal souls) in which many religious people believe. Materialism accepts naturalism but adds that the mental world that seems to be revealed through introspection is in fact nothing beyond the material states and processes that constitute our brains (and related nervous systems). Consciousness, for the materialist, is not another sort of natural reality—an immaterial sort—but the same sort of reality that we find in the external world: molecules, atoms, and whatever elementary particles make them up.

An atheist like Harris is a naturalist but not a materialist. He denies the gods and souls of religion but accepts the existence of mental states that are not reducible to matter. Science, he says, can describe these mental states, but it will have to be a science that accepts introspective reports as basic data that it must account for without redescribing them as brain states. Given what we know of neuroscience and evolution, consciousness somehow arose from unconscious matter. As Harris puts it: "First there is a physical world, unconscious and seething with unperceived events; then by virtue of some physical [material] property or process, consciousness itself springs, or staggers, into being" (56). He readily admits that the material world causes consciousness, but he denies that knowledge of its causes provides complete knowledge of the nature of consciousness. "Only consciousness can know itself—and directly, through first-person experience." It follows", he says, "that rigorous introspection . . . is an indispensable part of understanding the nature of the mind" (62).

Harris finds such rigorous introspection in Buddhist meditation, which he regards as a spiritual rather than a religious exercise. Here "spiritual" means that the meditation is directed toward learning about consciousness as a part of our natural experience, without any assumption or expectations of a reality beyond that experience. Harris is aware that even some Buddhists interpret their meditation as putting them into contact with supernatural deities, but he insists that the experience of consciousness in its own right reveals nothing supernatural.

What it does reveal, he claims, is the nonexistence of the self. This does not mean that there is no sense in which I exist. Rather, what "I" refers to is not, as many think, "the subject of experience", understood, for example, as "a thinker of thoughts inside one's head" or "an owner or inhabitant of a physical body" (92). Rather, "I" refers merely to the succession of particular experiences that introspection reveals, not to any continuing subject that has these experiences. (As Harris notes—n4, 227–28—this is David Hume's view in his *Treatise of Human Nature*.)

According to Harris, the nonexistence of the self "is an empirical claim: look closely enough at your own mind in the present moment, and you will discover that the self is an illusion" (92)—there's simply no such thing in your consciousness. Looking closely at our consciousness can, however, be difficult, given the distractions of the outside world and our deep-seated prejudice in favor of the self. But learning the techniques developed by Buddhist meditators can help us achieve "awakening". Further in accord with the Buddhist tradition, Harris sees escaping from the illusion of the self as the key to a life free from the selfish desires and fears that are the primary source of our unhappiness.

There are serious objections to Harris's position. Some would argue that atheism can't hold up without materialism, and others would claim that different methods of meditation lead to the affirmation of a self (in Hinduism) and even to a supernatural God (in Christianity). But for atheists who yearn for a spirituality they can't find in materialistic atheism, Buddhism as Harris understands it is a promising alternative.

11

RELIGION AND KNOWLEDGE

(KEITH DEROSE)

Keith DeRose is an expert on epistemology: the study of knowledge (*episteme* in Greek) and related notions. Here I offer some background to our discussion of the epistemology of religious belief.

The traditional philosophical definition of knowledge, going back to Plato's *Theaetetus*, is *justified true belief*: I know something (a claim, a statement, a proposition) if and only if I believe it, it is true, and I have a good justification for it. (Here I'm ignoring so-called Gettier counterexamples, which, though much discussed among philosophers, are seldom if ever relevant to real life.) It seems obvious that knowledge requires belief (roughly, thinking that something is true). If I don't even believe that God exists, I surely couldn't know it.

The idea that what we know must be true may seem less obvious. We often say things like "I just knew the Mets would win when they were up by four in the ninth inning, but they lost". We might regard this as a nonliteral use of "know". In any case, philosophers want to distinguish a use of "know" to express a high degree of subjective certainty ("I just knew . . .") from a use that asserts a claim as true. In this use of "know", a sentence such as "I know you are innocent, but you aren't" is a contradiction. This is the way DeRose and I will be using "know".

It might seem that we have knowledge when we have only true belief. But compare a man who believes his wife is unfaithful because of paranoid fantasies and a man who believes the same thing because of reports and photos from a reliable detective. Supposing that the wife does turn out to be unfaithful, we wouldn't say that the paranoid husband knew this, even though he believed it and it was true. Knowledge also requires some appropriate sort of justification.

But a belief can be justified without being true. Someone may have bribed the apparently reliable detective to falsify the report. Then, despite the high level of justification ("I had every reason to believe the detective"), it would not be true that the wife was unfaithful, and so it wouldn't be possible for the husband to know that she was. On the other hand, knowledge does not require certainty. We are justified in believing that there is no water on the moon, even though we aren't absolutely certain that some will not eventually be discovered. If in fact there is no water on the moon, we know this, in spite of the fact that our evidence doesn't exclude every chance of our being wrong. Knowledge requires only a reasonably high probability that a belief is true. Otherwise, we could not claim to know even the best-supported results of our science (for example, that the sun is millions of miles away from the Earth and much hotter than it).

Here, then, are some basics of epistemology: (1) Knowledge needs to be justified (we have to have good reasons for what we know); (2) the justification does not have to provide 100 percent certainty, just high probability; (3) what we know must, nonetheless, in fact be true.

Besides analyzing what's involved in knowledge, epistemologists are very interested in the right and wrong of believing. When am I entitled to believe something? When am I required to believe? When would it be wrong to believe? A first point to notice is that this talk of right and wrong need have nothing to do with morality. The questions are about what's right (or wrong) to do in the pursuit of knowledge. Sometimes, of course, knowledge (or at least justified belief) has moral significance. If I'm running an airline, I have a moral obligation to know whether my planes are safe. If I believe that they are safe but don't have good reason to think they are, then it's immoral for me to put them in the air, even if they are safe. On the other hand, if I have very good reason to believe they are safe, I can't be blamed for flying them, even if in fact they aren't safe. There may also be cases in which I have a moral duty to believe something without regard to whether it's true. If, for example, my hard-to-please best friend assures me that he loves the birthday present I gave him, I probably should believe what he says, without seeking solid reasons for its truth.

Epistemology, however, wants to know when I have a right to believe something when my goal is the truth. Here we run into an important point about truth: although a highly justified belief can turn out to be false, in practice, there is no difference between a highly justified belief and a true one.

Once I've gotten the strongest possible justification for a belief, there's nothing else I can do to find out if it's true (and, therefore, if I *really* know it). Justification is the only path to knowledge.

As a result, the epistemological question of whether I am right or wrong in believing something depends on my justification for the belief. In particular, my right to believe in God depends on whether I am justified in believing in God. At this point, some might object that everyone has a right to believe whatever they want to believe—it's a free country and we all have a right to our own opinions. But the "it's a free country" idea expresses a political (or moral) right to believe. It has nothing to do with our current question of whether I have good reason (justification) for my belief. You may have a moral right to believe that the Earth is flat, but you don't have an epistemological right to believe it.

DeRose and I also refer to two different forms of right or wrong belief. The justification for a belief may be strong enough to say that we ought to believe it—that it's wrong not to believe it. This would be the status of obvious everyday beliefs (for example, Chicago is usually colder in January than in July) and well-established scientific results (say, regarding the boiling points of liquids). But for other beliefs—such as controversial ethical and political convictions—we might have a right to believe without an obligation to do so. In some cases, the available evidence might give one person a right to believe a claim and another person a right to deny the same claim, depending on how each interprets the evidence.

Finally, there are important questions about what can amount to justification. (Talk of justification can be translated into talk about rationality: instead of saying a belief is *justified*, we can say that it's *rational*.) When we talk about justification we are often thinking about arguments (for example, a mathematical or scientific proof) for something we claim to know. An argument has premises—starting assumptions that are taken as clearly true—from which we can show that the claim (the conclusion) is—or very probably is—true. When the premises logically require that the conclusion be true, then the argument is deductive. When the premises merely make the conclusion highly probable, we have an inductive argument.

Arguments, however, are not by themselves able to justify a conclusion. They do so only if their premises are justified. Of course, we may be able to find further premises from which we can argue for the initial premises. I argue that Socrates is mortal from the premises "All humans are mortal" and "Socrates is human". Then I can further argue for "All humans are mortal" from the premise that we know of no humans from the distant past who have not died or from premises about human physiology. The problem, however, is that if accepting the premises of any argument requires further arguments, we will be caught in an infinite regress. We will have to keep giving proof after proof (for the premises of each successive argument) and so will never have justified anything.

The only solution to this problem is to find some premises that are justified *without an argument*. These are premises that we find so obviously true that they need no justification other than the fact that they seem so obvious. Sense perception (directly seeing, hearing, and so on) is one example: I'm justified in believing you're in the room with me because I see you. But there are also examples that involve a kind of mental seeing that has nothing to do with the senses: I just "see" that 3 is more than 2 or that it's wrong to torture babies for no reason. Plantinga's appeal to a *sensus divinitatis* in his interview is an example of a particularly controversial claim about the possibility of directly "seeing" that God exists. Much religious epistemology concerns what we can rightly claim is justified without a supporting argument.

INTERVIEW WITH KEITH DEROSE[*]

Gary Gutting: You've made the following statement: "Since atheists' only real hope of knowing that God doesn't exist would be through some kind of philosophical argument (perhaps some argument from evil), their knowing that God doesn't exist doesn't seem to me a very serious possibility" ("God's Existence and My Suspicion: Delusions of Knowledge", July 12, 2013, *The Prosbolgion* [online]).

I think many atheists would object that it's wrong to require them to have an argument showing that God doesn't exist. They'd claim their atheism is justified simply because there are no good arguments in favor of theism. After all, it's theists who are making an extraordinary claim. Isn't the lack of evidence for the claim that God exists sufficient grounds for denying it?

* This interview was originally published as "Why Take a Stance on God?" in *The Stone* (blog), *New York Times*, September 18, 2014.

Keith DeRose: I think you can sometimes rightly claim to know that something doesn't exist even if you don't have a good argument for your claim. This is the situation with the currently infamous Flying Spaghetti Monster: we all find it bizarre and literally unbelievable and so reject its existence without any argument. I, in fact, think some of our most important and interesting knowledge comes not through anything like arguments, but from just rightly rejecting as bizarre things that so strike us.

G.G.: Of course, what strikes us as bizarre can turn out to be true. It once seemed bizarre that the Earth was round, and that the Earth revolved around the sun.

K.D.: Right, but that just shows that what we once had good reason to think we knew can turn out to be false. It doesn't change the fact that, at a given time, the bizarreness of a belief may give us good reason for claiming that we know it's false.

In any case, the situation is very different with God. The thought that God exists does strike many atheists as bizarre. But in contrast to the Flying Spaghetti Monster, there are all of these theists and agnostics who do not find the thought of God's existence bizarre, and I really think they ruin our atheist friends' hopes for easy knowledge here. The basic point is that, when there are many other apparently sensible people who disagree with you, you need a good argument to claim that you know they're wrong.

G.G.: Are you saying that the mere fact that many disagree shows that we don't have knowledge? Most of us deny without argument the existence of the gods of many religions (the gods of the ancient Greeks and of contemporary voodoo, the pantheon of popular Hinduism). Don't we rightly claim to know these gods don't exist, although many have and do disagree?

K.D.: When your basis is not evidence or argument, but just how the matter strikes you, yes, the fact that the matter strikes others differently can undermine your claim to know. So, in particular, I am very skeptical about claims to know that the beliefs of major religions are false just because they strike us as bizarre.

If we knew that adherents to other religions came to hold their beliefs in some way that discredits them (say, through brainwashing), we might still know those beliefs are wrong on the basis of how bizarre they seem to us. Of course, there are probably some individual believers who have come to hold their beliefs in a way that discredits them. But we don't know enough about many believers to discredit their beliefs. So I don't think we can know they're wrong just because their beliefs strike us as bizarre.

G.G.: OK, maybe atheists can't rightly claim to know that theism is false just because they find it a bizarre claim. But atheists also point out that theists don't put forward any evidence for the existence of God that stands up to rational scrutiny. Isn't a total lack of evidence for a claim sufficient reason for denying it?

K.D.: No. When there's a genuine dispute, a lack of evidence on the other side does not give you knowledge if you don't have evidence for your claim.

G.G.: Of course, many atheists insist that they don't claim to *know* that there is no God. They at most maintain that God's existence is highly improbable, but don't claim absolute certainty that God doesn't exist. So, for example, if theists came up with good evidence for God, they might change their minds.

K.D.: My suggestion is that neither theists nor atheists *know* whether God exists. And here I don't just mean that they don't know for certain, but that they don't know at all.

It was about God, wasn't it, that Kant famously wrote "I had to deny knowledge in order to make room for faith"? Whatever it does or doesn't do for faith, my denial of knowledge here makes room for reasonable views on both sides of the question of whether God exists.

I don't think the arguments for either theism or atheism lead to knowledge of their conclusions. But there are arguments on both sides from premises that someone might reasonably judge to be plausible. If you find it quite probable that God does not exist, I think it's perfectly possible that you are reasonable to think as you do. But this doesn't mean that someone who thinks it is likely that God *does* exist can't likewise be reasonable in holding that position.

If you know that God does (or doesn't) exist, you

should be able to show that the best arguments for the opposite conclusion aren't ones that a reasonable person could find plausible. But to support that claim they would have to have better critiques of all those arguments than I've ever seen. In my view, it's more likely those who claim to know whether God exists—whether theists or atheists—are just blowing smoke.

G.G.: Without getting into details, could you mention a theistic and an atheistic argument that you think a reasonable person could find plausible?

K.D.: My favorite theistic example is the cosmological argument, particularly as William Rowe discusses it in his "Two Criticisms of the Cosmological Argument" (*The Monist*, 54 [1970], 441–59). This is the argument that tries to show that we need to posit God as the reason the universe exists. Negatively, it's clear to me that this argument does not really establish its conclusion. For it to work you have to accept a quite strong form of the Principle of Sufficient Reason (roughly, the claim that everything must have a reason). This principle is just too questionable for an argument based on it to produce knowledge. And, like Rowe, I in fact don't buy it.

But positively, given the state of the philosophical discussion, which has produced good responses to the apparently knockout objections, someone could certainly be reasonable in accepting the argument. This view has been cemented in place for me since I came to Yale, because my colleague Michael Della Rocca is a terrific, and very sensible, advocate of quite strong forms of the Principle of Sufficient Reason. He has never convinced me to join him in his rationalist ways, but because of him I would be willfully blind to think that even someone who understood the issue extremely well could not reasonably think as he does.

G.G.: How about an argument against God's existence?

K.D.: I'm going to have to be conventional here and go with the usual suspect: the argument from evil. Without getting to any details, you can feel the force of the argument choosing a suitably horrific example (the Holocaust, children dying of cancer) that leads you to say, "There's no way a perfectly good God would have allowed *that*!" There is a huge, often fascinating, discussion that tries to refute such arguments. But I find this intuitively powerful case does stand up to scrutiny, at the very least to the extent that someone could reasonably accept it at the end of the day. I suspect that even God thinks there is something wrong with you if you are not at least tempted by such an argument from evil.

G.G.: So far, you've argued that both atheists and theists can have good reasons for their views, so that neither side can rightly claim that the other is just irrational. But you make an important distinction between reasonably believing something and knowing that it's true, and you claim that neither atheists nor theists know whether God exists. Finally, what do you think of agnosticism, the view that, given the strong disagreement about theism, the most reasonable position is to remain undecided?

K.D.: In some ways, that view is right. One reading of "agnostic" is just "someone who does not take herself to know". On that reading, I accept the view. After all, my suggestion is that those who are not agnostics in that sense are deluded! But "agnostic" often slides into meaning something more along the lines of "someone who does not take a position on the issue, and is in that way 'undecided'", as you put it. And while I certainly think someone could easily be, and many people are, reasonable in being an agnostic about God in that stronger way, there are important goals served by our taking stands on issues where we cannot be objectively certain, or even know that we are right.

G.G.: Could you explain that more fully? If you don't know you're right, why take a stand?

K.D.: In philosophy and other areas of controversy, like politics, we often come to adopt a view on a disputed matter. When this happens, then even if you recognize the reasonableness of contrary views, you can come to really feel that your view is right, to the point that it can feel as if you know that it's true. And I think that taking such a strong stand on a disputed issue can be good. Those who take a strong stand may most effectively develop and defend their position. I don't think it would aid philosophy or politics if we all quickly abandoned our positions whenever we hit significant resistance from well-informed opponents. Often, that's just when things get interesting.

G.G.: But is the existence of God just a philosophical question, like, say, the definition of knowledge or the existence of Plato's forms?

K.D.: The existence of God is not just any philosophical issue. It's intimately tied up with what very many in our society feel gives meaning to their lives. As compared with other philosophical issues, many—including many professional philosophers—are especially protective of their position here. And on God's existence, I think many are subject to often subtle, but also often powerful, pressure from their religious groups to feel and to act and even to try to be certain of their position. This no doubt creates special dangers. But it also seems that a life of religious faith can lead us to special values we can't find elsewhere. . . . At any rate, this too is a philosophical issue. In light of all that, I would not want to make any blanket pronouncement, either about philosophers or people generally, that the most reasonable stance on the existence of God is to stay on the sidelines.

FURTHER THOUGHTS: KNOWLEDGE AND FAITH

Many religious people may well think the above discussion ignores the main factor behind their belief: faith. Religion, they will say, is not about rational justification but about a commitment that takes them to a truth beyond the grasp of mere reason.

But what can such a faith amount to? In ordinary life, faith is a way of believing without knowing. I don't directly know that the general theory of relativity and Fermat's Last Theorem are true; I know them by accepting the word of reliable experts—physicists and mathematicians. In fact, a little reflection reveals that a huge number of my beliefs—about science, history, countries I've never visited, people I don't know—are a matter of faith: belief on the word of others. Why should religion—which concerns things of which I have no direct knowledge—be any different?

However, our everyday human faith is based on knowledge relayed by various people who have direct information on these topics. In fact, I can rightly be said to know, although indirectly, because I'm justified in believing that the people I rely on are honestly telling me what they know. If I try to justify religious belief in this way, I have to appeal to the reliability of what my church's leaders or teachers tell me. But what reason do I have to think that they have knowledge of divine truth? At best, they can claim that they have received this knowledge from God himself (or from others to whom God has revealed the truth). Here God becomes the reliable source of truth. As in the case of everyday faith, this appeal takes the form of an argument: God is a reliable authority; God says that the claims of religion are true, so it is rational to believe these claims. But such an appeal assumes that there *is* a God—a fundamental religious claim that would itself have to be known by faith, if faith is to play the role of knowledge in the justification of religion. So the idea that religious faith is analogous to everyday human faith leads to a circle: I believe in God because God assures me that he exists.

A more promising move is to think of faith as a belief not justified by any argument, not even an argument from authority, but as a belief that is justified without argument. (Recall Alvin Plantinga's support of this view.) Many of our most important beliefs simply arise in the course of our lives, with no argumentative support. In our discussion of Plantinga, we saw how this is true of the belief that other people have subjective experiences. Another example is our belief that what has happened in the past is often a reliable guide to what will happen in the future—that, for example, the sun will rise tomorrow because it has always done so. But we have no good argument for this claim. The best most of us could do is to say that, in the past, the past has often been a good guide to the future—but, as David Hume pointed out, that is a totally circular argument. The fact is that we are entitled to believe this and similar claims without any argument—they just seem obvious. If this is the way the existence of God seems to me—unprovable by argument but obviously true—what's wrong with my believing in God?

I'm not defending this way of justifying religious belief. It faces many difficulties, some of which are suggested by my discussion with DeRose. My point here is just that this approach is probably the best way of understanding what religious people mean when they say they believe on faith.

12

A HISTORICAL CONTEXT

(DANIEL GARBER)

My last interviewee is Daniel Garber, a historian of philosophy in what is called the modern period, from the seventeenth to the nineteenth centuries. Our interview tries to put the contemporary question of religious belief into the context of the three preceding centuries. This context is important because the basic issues have shifted since the dawn of modernity.

At the heart of the change, as Garber explains, was a reversal of polarity between theism and atheism. In seventeenth-century Europe, almost everyone—including the most innovative intellectuals such as Galileo, Locke, and Descartes—were Christians. Atheism was seen as a threat, but the threat, if it existed, was well hidden. Garber explores some of the possible causes of this reversal but finds no simple explanation. In particular, he insists that the new science (and the philosophy accompanying it) did not refute theism. Theism remained an intellectually viable position, even if new scientific discoveries

required believers to abandon or reinterpret some traditional beliefs. Garber himself is an atheist, although he says
he would be open to belief if he found a convincing line of
theistic argument.

The interview ends with a discussion of Pascal's famous
wager argument. This is an appropriate finale to the series,
since the wager was Pascal's last, desperate attempt to argue
the nonbeliever to faith in God.

Blaise Pascal was a seventeenth-century French mathematician and philosopher, who, among much else, helped
develop mathematical probability and decision theory. His
work originated in response to a puzzle about how to bet on a
dice game. But it also suggested an argument that believing in
God is a good bet at any odds, since the possible payoff—eternal happiness—far outweighs any costs of believing—even of
believing in a God who does not exist.

More fully, the argument starts from the fact that there
is no avoiding the choice between *believing that there is a God*
and *not believing that there is a God*. If there is no decisive evidence available to decide this issue, we must make what the-
orists call a *decision under uncertainty*; we must decide which
choice to make when we don't know which will turn out to
be correct. Decision theory tells us we need to take account
of two things: the probability that our choice will be correct
and the value of a correct choice. This, of course, is what the
gambler must decide when placing a bet: is the return if I
win worth the risk of losing? Pascal claims that if I believe in
God and he turns out to exist, then my gain is infinite (that
is, happiness forever in heaven), whereas if I believe in him
and he doesn't exist, my loss will only be finite (I lose only

the pleasures and so forth that religion might require me to renounce for the limited span of my life). Here the choice should be obvious: the possibility of an infinite gain (no matter how unlikely) is worth any finite risk. As Pascal puts it: "If you win, you win everything; if you lose, you lose nothing" (*Pensées*, #233).

There are many criticisms of Pascal's reasoning. Some note the apparent impossibility of simply choosing to believe what you don't believe: you could offer me a million dollars to believe right now that I'm on the moon, but I couldn't do it. Others worry about the intellectual dishonesty of believing without evidence or the calculating self-interest of those who follow the argument just to get to heaven (wouldn't those be just the people God would not want?). Still others note that, although Pascal applies the argument only to belief in the Christian God, it would in fact apply to the god or gods of any religion. Different religions require mutually conflicting beliefs, and I can't believe what I know are contradictions. Garber, as we shall see, finds Pascal's argument attractive but rejects it on grounds of intellectual integrity.

INTERVIEW WITH DANIEL GARBER[*]

Gary Gutting: In the seventeenth century most philosophers were religious believers, whereas today most seem to be atheists. What explains this reversal?

---

[*] This interview was originally published as "Can Wanting to Believe Make Us Believers?" in *The Stone* (blog), *New York Times*, October 5, 2014.

Daniel Garber: I think that it is fair to say that in the seventeenth century most people, not just philosophers, were believers and that it was simply taken for granted that people of ordinary intelligence would believe in God, in just the way that people today take it for granted that people of ordinary intelligence have faith in the authority of science. Many important scientists and mathematicians in the period were also believers, including Bacon, Descartes, Boyle, Pascal, and Newton. Not that there weren't atheists in the period, but atheism was something that in many circles needed a special explanation in a way in which belief didn't.

In many circumstances, atheism was considered so obviously contrary to evident reason, that there had to be a special explanation for why atheists denied what was so obvious to most of their contemporaries, in much the way that today we might wonder about those who deny science. What changed? I hesitate even to speculate. There was the Enlightenment, the Industrial Revolution, political revolutions, Darwinism, the wars of the twentieth century, a lot. As a result science and religious faith have, in a way, exchanged places, and a general and widespread faith in science has replaced the earlier general and widespread faith in God. But even so, God is not dead among the philosophers. There is still a very significant community of believers among philosophers. I'm personally not one of them, I should say, and I would doubt that they constitute a majority. But even so, I think they cannot be ignored.

G.G.: What you've described could be taken as a social and cultural change that says nothing about the truth of religious claims. Contemporary atheists often say that the development of science since the seventeenth century has undermined the intellectual basis of theism. What do you think?

D.G.: Unlike some, I would hesitate to say that modern science has *refuted* religion in any strong sense. Religion and theology are complicated and subtle; they cannot easily be refuted. In the past religion has confronted a variety of scientific challenges, from the rediscovery of ancient scientific systems like Aristotle's in the twelfth and thirteenth centuries to Copernicus, Galileo, Descartes, and Newton in the sixteenth and seventeenth centuries to Darwin in the nineteenth and beyond. These discoveries have forced religion to adapt in various ways, but those contemporary advocates of religion who are, in my opinion, the most sophisticated don't feel that they have to oppose science in order to keep their faith.

For some this adaptability is a sign that religion is empty, on the assumption that to be meaningful religion must be falsifiable. But I don't agree. Philosophers of science have rightly rejected naïve falsificationism, and it shouldn't be accepted in the philosophy of religion. Again, I am not a believer. But even so, I don't underestimate how difficult it is to refute theism.

G.G.: "Naïve falsification" is the idea that a theory should be rejected as soon as one of its implications is shown to be false. In fact, scientists rightly allow revising a theory to avoid falsifications, but only if the revised theory eventually makes new predictions that might be falsified. What science doesn't allow is continual revision to avoid any and every refutation. But isn't that just what religious believers do, resulting in what the twentieth-century English philosopher Antony Flew called religion's "death by a thousand qualifications"? Is there any evidence that believers would accept as refuting their position?

D.G.: I'm not a believer, so I'm not in a position to say. First of all, it's worth noting that some of the biggest empirical challenges don't come from science but from common features of life. Perhaps the hardest case for believers is the Problem of Evil, the question of how a benevolent God could allow the existence of evil in the world—both natural evils like devastating earthquakes and human evils like the Holocaust—has always been a great challenge to faith in God. There is, of course, a long history of responses to that problem that goes back to Job. While nonbelievers (like me) consider this a major problem, believers have, for the most part, figured out how to accommodate themselves to it.

But science offers challenges as well. For some who believe in the literal truth of the Bible, for example, discovering that the Bible contains claims that are literally false would have to lead to a crisis of faith, or, perhaps more likely, to a rejection of scientific claims. But for more sophisticated believers I suspect that the claims of religion are more like broad structural principles that can be reinterpreted as we learn more about the world. In physics, one might be reluctant to give up broad structural ideas like the existence of general conservation principles, even when some localized experimental evidence may seem to go against them. In that circumstance one might choose to keep the broad and well-entrenched principles and figure out how to reinterpret them so as to fit with experience. I think that some believers may consider the existence of God in something of the same way. But, again, I don't say any of this with a lot of confidence since I am not a member of the community of believers.

G.G.: What do you see as the current status of traditional metaphysical arguments for God's existence? Are they of merely historical interest?

D.G.: Good question. It is, in fact, a good question why they were so widespread in the history of philosophy. Not every theist—then or now—would necessarily think that arguments for the existence of God are necessary, or even possible. And if belief in God were generally taken for granted, as it was in the seventeenth century, then trying to prove the existence of God would seem to be an unnecessary exercise. But at various times and places in that century there were genuine anxieties about the existence of these mythical atheists, and perhaps we should understand the arguments in that context.

Marin Mersenne, Descartes's close friend and sponsor, and an important mathematician and scientific thinker in his own right, claimed that there were over 50,000 atheists living in Paris in 1623. In his massive commentary on Genesis, where he advanced that claim, he offered thirty-five arguments for the existence of God. For Mersenne and his contemporaries, the idea of the atheist was terrifying. Many thought that, without the threat of divine punishment, there was no reason for people to act morally. Establishing the rationality of belief in God had high stakes for them.

Today, those who don't believe, philosophers and others, don't seem to pay much attention to the contemporary literature on proofs for the existence of God. Proofs for the existence of God have become something of an empty intellectual enterprise, I'm afraid.

G.G.: So are you saying that the philosophical books are closed on the traditional theistic arguments? Have atheistic philosophers decisively shown that the arguments fail, or have they merely ceased thinking seriously about them?

D.G.: Certainly there are serious philosophers who would deny that the arguments for the existence of God have been decisively refuted. But even so, my impression is that proofs for the existence of God have ceased to be a matter of serious discussion outside of the domain of professional philosophy of religion. And even there, my sense is that the discussions are largely a matter of academic interest: the real passion has gone out of the question.

G.G.: I wonder if the lack of passion reflects the fact that centuries of discussion have not yielded any decisive conclusion about whether the arguments work. That, I think, would support an agnostic rather than an atheistic conclusion. On the other hand, many contemporary atheists reject theism on the grounds that there is simply no serious case that has been made for God's existence. As a historian of philosophy (and an atheist), what's your view on this issue?

D.G.: Centuries of discussion have certainly not led to a consensus about the arguments. But we cannot forget that at some times in the past, there was a general consensus that God exists, and, perhaps, a general (though not universal) consensus that some of the arguments, for example the argument from a first cause, are correct. The question is really why arguments that were once convincing have lost their power, something that is true of many arguments from the history of philosophy.

I think, though, that the lack of passion reflects more than anything else the cultural change that has made faith and religion less central to our lives, since at least the Enlightenment. This has left the concern to prove the existence of God to people of faith who are concerned with the intellectual grounds of faith, that is, largely philosophers who are believers, philosophers of religion, and theologians. You are right to say that many contemporary atheists reject theism because they see no convincing reason to believe. While I am by no means dismissive of religion, that's where I would place myself.

G.G.: In your essay in Louise Antony's collection *Philosophers Without Gods*, you say, "Much as I try, much as I may want to, I cannot be a believer." Why can't you—and why would you want to?

D.G.: I can't believe because I'm not convinced that it is true that God exists. It is as simple as that. Belief is not voluntary, and there are no (rational) considerations that move me to believe that God exists. In all honesty, I will admit that I don't have a definitive argument that God *doesn't* exist either. Which is to say that I refuse to make the judgment that some make that it is positively irrational to believe in God in an objective sense. But without convincing affirmative reasons to believe, I'm stuck. If others find reasons that convince them, I'm willing to discuss them and consider them. Who knows? There might be a convincing argument out there, or at least, one that convinces me.

On the other hand, it is easy to say why I might *want* to believe. I see people around me—often very smart and thoughtful people—who get great comfort from believing that God exists. Why wouldn't I want to be like them? It's just that I can't.

G.G.: Wanting to believe in God suggests Pascal's wager argument, which remains for many the most appealing case for religious belief. What do you think about it?

D.G.: Formally, the argument has many well-known flaws, though it also has its friends. Even knowing the flaws, I do find myself somewhat moved by it. The reason is that at the core of the argument there are some very compelling intuitions. Basically, the argument turns on the idea that if there is a God, and we believe in him, we then have a shot at eternal happiness. If God doesn't exist, then we are stuck in this very finite and imperfect life, whether we believe in him or not. So, it would seem, for all sorts of reasons, we should want to believe in him. The problem (perhaps insuperable) is taking these plausible considerations and turning them into a genuine argument.

But the real worry about the argument comes at a later moment, I think. It is important to remember that Pascal's wager isn't an argument for the truth of the proposition that God exists, but an argument for why we should *want* to believe that God exists: it only tells us that it is to our advantage to believe, and in this way makes us want to believe, but it doesn't give us any *reasons* to think that God actually exists. In a way, I'm already convinced that I should *want* to believe. But there is a step from there to actual belief, and that's a step I cannot personally negotiate. Pascal tells us, roughly, that we should adopt the life of the believer and eventually the belief will come. And maybe it will. But that seems too much like self-deception to me.

G.G.: You seem to be ignoring what is often taken as the heart of Pascal's argument: a cost-benefit calculation that you should believe in God because the likely benefits of belief are greater than the likely benefits of nonbelief. Put that way, the argument seems morally dubious, leading to William James's comment that God would likely exclude from heaven precisely the sorts of people who believe because of such an argument. Is this a misreading of Pascal?

D.G.: That objection doesn't really move me. Pascal's wager is certainly a cost-benefit argument. But as I noted earlier, the important thing is what happens afterward. If behaving like a believer transforms you and causes the scales to fall from your eyes, and allows you to appreciate the existence of God in a way that you couldn't before, when you resisted belief, then why should God complain? In any case, we are not in a very good position to figure out what God might judge on such an issue—if, indeed, there is a God. But what worries me more than what God might think is the possibility that I may corrupt my soul by deceiving myself into believing something, just because I want it to be true. For a philosopher, that's a kind of damnation in this life.

FURTHER THOUGHTS: PASCAL 2.0

Maybe Pascal's wager aims too high by trying to convince a nonbeliever to believe. That may have been a plausible ambition in the seventeenth century. But today, when doubt rather than belief seems to be the default position, it might make more sense to adapt the argument to argue that agnosticism is preferable to atheism. Here's my effort in this direction.

The wager requires a choice between believing and not believing. But there are two ways of not believing. I can either deny that God exists or doubt that God exists. Discussions of the wager usually follow Pascal and lump these two together in the single option of not believing in God. They don't distinguish denying from doubting because both are ways of not believing. The argument then is about whether believing is a better option than not believing. My formulation of the argument will focus instead on the choice between denying and doubting God.

Denial of God means that I simply close the door on the hope that there is something beyond the natural world; doubt may keep that door open. I say "may" because doubt can express indifference to what is doubted: I don't know and I don't care whether there is an even number of stars or whether there are planets made of purple rock. Indifferent doubt is the practical equivalent of denial, since both refuse to take a given belief as a viable possibility—neither sees it as what William James called a "live option". But doubt may also be open to and even desirous of what it doubts. I may doubt that I will ever understand and appreciate Pierre Boulez's music, but still hope that I someday will.

I propose to reformulate Pascal's wager as urging those who doubt God's existence to embrace a doubt of desire rather than a doubt of indifference. This means, first, that they should hope—and therefore desire—that they might find a higher meaning and value to their existence by making contact with a beneficent power beyond the natural world. There's no need to further specify the nature of this power in terms, say, of the teachings of a particular religion.

The argument begins by noting that we could be much happier by making appropriate contact with such a power. The next question is whether there are paths we can take that have some prospect of achieving this contact. Many people, including some of the most upright, intelligent, and informed, have claimed that there are such paths. These include not just rituals and good deeds but also private spiritual exercises of prayer, meditation, and even philosophical speculation. A person's specific choices would depend on individual inclinations and capacities.

So far, then, we have good reason to expect much greater happiness if there is a beneficent power we could contact, and we know of paths that might lead to that contact. The only remaining question is whether there are negative effects of seeking God that would offset the possible (but perhaps very improbable) value of contact with God.

Unlike the traditional versions, this wager does not require believing that there is a God. So Garber's worries about self-deception or insincerity don't arise. The wager calls for some manner of spiritual commitment, but there is no demand for belief, either immediately or eventually. The commitment is, rather, to what I will call *religious agnosticism*: serious involvement with religious teachings and practices, in hope for a truth that I do not have and may never attain. Further, religious agnosticism does not mean that I renounce all claims to other knowledge. I may well have strong commitments to scientific, philosophical, and ethical truths that place significant constraints on the religious approaches I find appropriate. Religious agnosticism demands only that I reject atheism, which excludes the hope for something beyond the natural world knowable by science.

Religious agnosticism may accept the ethical value of a religious way of living and even endorse religious ideas as a viable basis for understanding various aspects of human existence. But the ethical value is a matter of my own judgment, independent of religious authority. And the understanding may be only a partial illumination that does not establish the ultimate truth of the ideas that provide it. For example, both Dante and Proust help us understand the human condition, despite their conflicting intellectual frameworks. None of this will interfere with a commitment to intellectual honesty.

But perhaps a "serious involvement" with religion will require giving up other humanly fulfilling activities to make room for religious thought and action. Given a low likelihood of attaining a "higher" form of happiness, it may make more sense to seek only the "worldly" satisfactions that are more certain, even if less profound. But we can decide for ourselves how much worldly satisfaction is worth giving up for the sake of possible greater spiritual happiness. And it may well turn out that religious activities such as meditation and charitable works have their own significant measure of worldly satisfaction. Given all this, what basis is there for refusing the wager?

I don't see this new wager as merely a way of nudging atheists and indifferent agnostics onto a religious path. It's also important for those who are committed to a religious community to realize that such commitment doesn't require believing the teachings of that community. It's enough to see those teachings—and the practices connected with them—as a good starting point for an inquiry into their truth. We should also realize that the real truth of a religion may be quite different from its official "self-understanding" of this truth. A living religion should have room both for believers at ease with its official teachings and for nonbelievers (religious agnostics) who see these teachings as a promising beginning in their search for the truth.

I don't claim that my version of the wager argument is a faithful explication of what Pascal had in mind. It is, rather, an adaptation of the argument to our intellectual context, where atheists who resist theism as an irrational dogma, might still worry that a vigorous denial of God might itself be dogmatic. But I do think that this version avoids the standard objections to the usual interpretations of the wager argument. It does not require belief and isn't an attempt to trick God into sending us to heaven. It merely calls us to follow a path that has some chance of leading us to an immensely important truth.

By Way of a Conclusion

*F*inally, *I offer a personal reflection on the preceding twelve interviews. In the interviews, I often suggested views and objections that don't express my own commitments in an effort to clarify or deepen my interviewees' positions. Here I try to express my own ideas, without suggesting that they are the only reasonable response to the issues we've been discussing. It seemed natural to keep to the interview format, even though I (G.G.) had no one to interview except myself (g.g.). I've tried to submit myself to what I hope was the polite but challenging voice questioning my interviewees.*

G.G.: What was the point of talking to a bunch of philosophers about religious belief?

g.g.: The immediate impetus came from the poll I cited at the beginning of the first interview: 73 percent of

---

* This "interview" was originally published as "Debating God: Notes on an Unanswered Question" in *The Stone* (blog), *New York Times*, October 13, 2014.

philosophers said they accepted or were inclined to atheism, while 15 percent accepted or inclined to theism. Only around 6 percent identified themselves as agnostics. I would have expected a good majority to identify as agnostics.

G.G.: Why was that?

g.g.: The question of whether God exists is a controversial one: there have been, and still are, lots of smart, informed, and sincere people on both sides. So it would seem that philosophers, committed to rational reflection on the big questions, wouldn't be atheists (or theists) without good reasons. But it is also obvious that the standard arguments for and against God's existence—first-cause arguments, the Problem of Evil, and so on—have stimulated an enormous amount of debate, leading to many complications but to no consensus. Given this, it seemed to me that at least a good proportion of philosophers would be agnostics, undecided about God's existence.

G.G.: So you wanted to talk to philosophers to see why they accepted or denied the existence of God. What did you find out?

g.g.: Well, the theists were pretty much as I expected. None claimed to have a decisive argument for God's existence; that is, an argument they thought should convince any reasonable person. Alvin Plantinga claimed that there are lots of "pretty good" arguments, but allowed that they aren't conclusive, even though they may be "as good as philosophical arguments get"— which I take to mean that they can make it rational to assert God's existence, but don't make it irrational to deny it.

Sajjad Rizvi suggests something similar when he says that theistic proofs "allow believers to fit their faith in God into a rationally coherent framework", even though atheists may not find them rationally compelling. But two other theists, John Caputo (a Catholic) and Howard Wettstein (a Jew) think that arguing for God's existence misunderstands what religion is all about.

In my experience, all this is typical of philosophers who believe in God. As Daniel Garber noted, once upon a time believing philosophers thought they had arguments showing that atheism was irrational. Nowadays, most of them merely argue that it can be rational to be a theist.

G.G.: And the atheists? Are they interested in refuting theistic arguments or providing arguments that God doesn't exist?

g.g.: Not especially. Citing Garber again: "Today, those who don't believe, philosophers and others, don't seem to pay much attention to the contemporary literature on proofs for the existence of God. [Such proofs] have become something of an empty intellectual enterprise". Atheist philosophers do often refer to the argument from evil, but, like Louise Antony and Michael Ruse, they say little more than that they personally find it convincing. Atheists generally don't claim that those who reject the argument are irrational, and very few seem to have looked closely at the extensive and highly technical current literature on the question. Philip Kitcher expressed a common view when he said he had "little sympathy for strained discussions" about God and evil.

G.G.: So are you saying that the atheists don't have any good arguments?

g.g.: No, they do, but they're against specific forms of religious belief. There's a very strong case—nicely developed by Tim Maudlin in our interview—against arguing for the existence of God (in any religiously relevant sense) as a scientific hypothesis. And Kitcher gave a powerful formulation of the case against believing the doctrines of a *particular faith*. The point is that there's often no more reason for believing those doctrines (say, the triune nature of God, God becoming man, the Last Judgment) than there is for believing those of other faiths. Therefore, if you deny the doctrines of other faiths, then you should also deny the doctrines of your faith.

G.G.: You don't think philosophical believers have good responses to those arguments?

g.g.: No, but few of them hold the positions the arguments refute. First of all, they don't think saying that

God exists is a scientific claim. On the contrary, they think it's a claim that there is something beyond the scope of scientific investigation and testing. They may think it's knowable by metaphysical arguments or (more likely) by religious experiences. But they don't think either metaphysics or religious experiences are part of scientific inquiry.

G.G.: Many atheists will say that such mental gymnastics are just rationalizations of an emotional need for religion, that if believers faced up to the evolutionary and psychological facts that explain beliefs, they could slough off their childish delusions.

g.g.: The weakest intellectual aspect of current atheism is its naïve enchantment with pseudoscientific biological and psychological explanations of why people believe. There are no doubt all sorts of disreputable sources for religious belief, and the same goes for rejections of religion. But it's just silly to say that there's solid scientific evidence that religious belief in general has causes that undermine its claims to truth. Here I think Louise Antony was right on target: "Theists are insulted by such conjectures (which is all they are) and I don't blame them. It's presumptuous to tell someone else why she believes what she believes—if you want to know, start by *asking her.*"

G.G.: OK, but at least aren't believers who appeal to religious experience and metaphysical arguments admitting what popular atheism so insistently claims: there's simply no evidence for God's existence, and that alone warrants atheism?

g.g.: There's no *scientific* evidence, but there are other sorts of evidence.

G.G.: I suspect that most atheists think scientific evidence, evidence that ultimately appeals only to empirically observable facts, is the only sort of evidence there is.

g.g.: That may be their assumption, but how do they show that it's correct? It certainly isn't supported by scientific evidence, since that tells us about only what *is* empirically observable. The question is whether there is anything else.

G.G.: Well, at least atheists can try to show that the allegedly nonscientific evidence that theists put forward doesn't support their conclusion. They can, for example, argue that the religious experiences are illusory and the metaphysical arguments are unsound.

g.g.: Agreed, but then they have to show that. They can't just keep saying "There's no empirical evidence" and think they've shown that a theism based on metaphysical reasoning or nonempirical experience is irrational. The core question is whether there is anything beyond the empirical—some transcendent reality we can call God. I don't think that it's irrational to say there isn't a transcendent reality. But to show that it's irrational to say that there is, you'd have to end the impasse in philosophical discussions of theism. That's where atheism falls short and agnosticism is the preferable position.

What I'm saying about religion is what many rightly say about other strongly disputed areas, such as ethics and politics: people on both sides can be reasonable in holding their positions, but neither side has a basis for saying that their opponents are irrational. This, I think, was what Keith DeRose was getting at when he said that no one knows whether or not God exists.

G.G.: Fair enough, but the unsettled discussions are only about the existence of a minimal god (say an intelligent and benevolent creator). That falls far short of what most religions believe about their gods. And as you've noted, Kitcher's argument shows that the sorts of reasons believers have for rejecting the distinctive doctrines of other religions will tell against their own doctrines.

g.g.: That's a major problem for believers who are exclusivist about their doctrines. The best response, I think, is to insist that any concepts we apply to God fall far short of grasping the divine reality. If so, then we should expect that different, even apparently contradictory, claims about God could all be true. In fact, you don't even need rival faiths to think this way. Christianity has from early on wrestled with apparent contradictions in its own doctrines. How can there be just one God but three divine persons? How can Christ be both wholly divine and wholly human? Thomas Aquinas and many others have offered ingenious and often illuminating accounts of how to make sense of such claims. But the ultimate appeal to mystery remains inevitable.

G.G.: So what you're saying is that, in the face of atheist criticisms, religious belief can still be rational, but only if it gives up thinking of the existence of God as a scientific hypothesis and admits that many of its claims are fundamentally mysterious. Doesn't that in fact undermine most of traditional religious belief?

g.g.: It's more accurate to say that it undermines a strong tendency of religion—at least in its major monotheistic forms—to misunderstand its own basic message. There's nothing in the Bible that presents God as a well-confirmed scientific hypothesis, and there's a great deal that emphasizes that the truths of religion are beyond human comprehension. In spite of this, believers too often play the double game of insisting on God's transcendence and mystery to meet rational objections, but then acting as if they'd justified a straightforward literal understanding of their beliefs.

G.G.: So are you what we might call a "mysterian theist"?

g.g.: No, I'm an agnostic. I don't find it reasonable to accept or reject a transcendent God, so I withhold judgment.

G.G.: How can you be an agnostic and still claim to be a Catholic?

g.g.: Because, despite my agnosticism, I still think it's worth pursuing the question of whether God exists, and for me the Catholic intellectual and cultural tradition has the most value in that pursuit. People with other backgrounds will quite rightly find another religion (or aspects of several religions) the best locus for their search.

G.G.: Still, I don't see how you can find a place in a Church that claims to be the custodian of a divine revelation, when you don't believe in that revelation.

g.g.: The fundamental "revelation" is the moral ideal expressed in the biblical account of Christ's life. Whether or not that account is historically accurate, the New Testament Christ remains an exemplar of an impressive ideal. Engagement with the practices (ethical and liturgical) inspired by that ideal is, to my mind, sufficient for being a Catholic. Beyond that, historical narratives and theological doctrines can at least function as useful means of understanding, even for those who aren't prepared to say that they are true in any literal sense. Some believers may have experiences (or even arguments) that have convinced them that these doctrines are true. But religions—even Catholicism—should have room for those who don't see it that way.

G.G.: So it seems that you agree with most of your interviewees—believers and nonbelievers—that practice is more important than doctrine.

g.g.: Yes, and I agree with Kitcher that the greatest obstacle facing atheism is its lack of the strong communal practices that characterize religions. People need to believe something that provides a satisfying way of living their lives, and most people need to find this in a community. So far atheism has produced nothing like the extensive and deep-rooted communities of belief that religion has.

G.G.: But as atheists often point out, religions themselves often lead to barbarous behavior.

g.g.: That's because religious faith without a strong role for critical reason readily falls into fanaticism. I thought this was one lesson of my interview with Sajjad Rizvi. He showed the historical connection of Islam with traditions of philosophical reflection that have tempered excesses of blind faith. Although such traditions are still effective in many parts of the Muslim world, it's undeniable that there are places where they have failed and a fanatical mutation has gone out of control.

G.G.: What about the stunning moral failings of your own church? Don't they show a fundamental corruption that requires abandoning it?

g.g.: The corruption largely arises from failing to give practice the religious priority it deserves. The Catholic Church lets indefensible doctrines about papal infallibility and hierarchical authority interfere with its fundamental ethics of love. A sensible change on birth control, forbidden only because it would admit fallibility, would help the poor and probably do more than anything else to prevent abortions. And the cover-ups of sex abuse were largely driven by a fear of weakening clerical authority. The best response is not to withdraw but to work for a new Reformation to dislodge the doctrines and practices that undermine the fundamental mission of the Church.

About the Interviewees

Louise Antony is professor of philosophy at the University of Massachusetts Amherst. Her main areas of research are philosophy of mind, epistemology, feminist theory, and philosophy of religion, and she has published scores of articles in these areas. She was the coeditor (with Charlotte Witt) of *A Mind of One's Own: Feminist Essays on Reason and Objectivity* and (with Norbert Hornstein) *Chomsky and His Critics*. More recently, she was the editor of *Philosophers Without Gods: Reflections on Atheism and the Secular Life*, published by Oxford University Press. She has served as president of the Society for Philosophy and Psychology and as president of the Eastern Division of the American Philosophical Association.

John D. Caputo, the Thomas J. Watson Professor of Religion Emeritus (Syracuse University) and the David R. Cook Professor of Philosophy Emeritus (Villanova University), writes and lectures in the area of postmodern theory and theology. His latest books are *Hoping Against Hope: Confessions of a Postmod-*

ern Pilgrim; *The Folly of God: A Theology of the Unconditional*; *The Insistence of God: A Theology of Perhaps*; and *Truth: Philosophy in Transit*.

Keith DeRose is the Allison Foundation Professor of Philosophy at Yale University. His main areas of research are epistemology, philosophy of language, and philosophy of religion. He is the author of *The Case for Contextualism*, the recently completed but not-yet-published *The Appearance of Ignorance*, and many papers in his areas of interest.

Jonardon Ganeri's books include *The Self: Naturalism, Consciousness, and the First-Person Stance*; *The Lost Age of Reason: Philosophy in Early Modern India 1450–1700*; *The Concealed Art of the Soul*; and *Philosophy in Classical India: The Proper Work of Reason*. He is currently editing the *Oxford Handbook of Indian Philosophy*, preparing a monograph on consciousness and attention in Buddhism and cognitive science, and drafting scripts about Indian philosophy for the podcast *History of Philosophy Without any Gaps*. He is a Fellow of the British Academy, and winner of the 2015 Infosys Prize in the Humanities.

Daniel Garber (PhD, Harvard, 1975) is Stuart Professor of Philosophy at Princeton University, and associated faculty in the Program in the History of Science and the Department of Politics. Garber specializes in the history of philosophy and science in the early-modern period, and is also interested in issues in epistemology and the philosophy of science. In addition to numerous articles, Garber is the author of *Descartes's Metaphysical Physics*; *Descartes Embodied*; *Leibniz: Body,*

Substance, Monad and is the coeditor (with Michael Ayers) of *The Cambridge History of Seventeenth-Century Philosophy.*

Jay Garfield is Kwan Im Thong Hood Cho Temple Professor of Humanities and head of studies in Philosophy at Yale-NUS College; professor of philosophy at the National University of Singapore; recurrent visiting professor of philosophy at Yale University; Doris Silbert Professor in the Humanities and professor of philosophy at Smith College; professor of philosophy at Melbourne University; and adjunct professor of philosophy at the Central University of Tibetan Studies. Garfield's most recent books include *Engaging Buddhism: Why It Matters to Philosophy*; *Moonpaths: Ethics and Emptiness* (with the Cowherds, Oxford, 2015); and with James Henle and Thomas Tymoczko, *Sweet Reason: A Field Guide to Modern Logic*, 2nd Edition.

Philip Kitcher is currently the John Dewey Professor of Philosophy at Columbia University. He is the author of sixteen books and a large number of articles on a wide range of philosophical topics. A former president of the Pacific Division of the American Philosophical Association, he was the first recipient of the association's Prometheus Prize for work in expanding the frontiers of science and philosophy. The most recent of his books, *Life After Faith: The Case for Secular Humanism*, develops the themes of his Terry Lectures delivered at Yale University in the spring of 2013.

Tim Maudlin holds a BA in physics and philosophy from Yale University and a PhD in history and philosophy of science from the University of Pittsburgh. He taught philosophy at Rutgers University for twenty-five years, and moved to New York University in 2011. He studies the nature of space and time, as well as quantum theory. His most recent work develops a new mathematical language for describing the structure of space and time.

Alvin Plantinga is the inaugural William Harry Jellema Professor of Christian Philosophy at Calvin College, as well as emeritus John A. O'Brien Professor of Philosophy at the University of Notre Dame. Among his books are *God and Other Minds*; *The Nature of Necessity*; *Warrant and Proper Function*; *Warranted Christian Belief*; and *Where the Conflict Really Lies: Science, Religion, and Naturalism.*

Sajjad Rizvi is director of the Institute of Arab and Islamic Studies and associate professor of Islamic intellectual history at the University of Exeter. He specializes in Islamic thought and hermeneutics in the early-modern period and is currently writing a book on Islamic philosophy in the East during the pivotal eighteenth century.

Michael Ruse is Lucyle T. Werkmeister Professor of Philosophy and director of the Program in the History and Philosophy of Science at Florida State University. A Fellow of the Royal Society of Canada, he has held a Guggenheim Fellowship and was a Gifford Lecturer. The founding editor of the journal *Biology and Philosophy*, he has written or edited more than fifty books as well as professional and more popular articles, including a piece (on science and religion) for *Playboy*. *Darwinism as Religion: What Literature Tells Us About Evolution* will appear in 2016, to be published by Oxford University Press.

Howard Wettstein's BA was from Yeshiva University, 1965; PhD City University of New York, 1976. He is currently professor of philosophy at UC Riverside. Previously he held positions at the University of Notre Dame and the University of Minnesota, Morris, and visiting positions at Stanford University and the University of Iowa. His main research areas are the philosophy of religion and the philosophy of language. He has been the editor of *Midwest Studies in Philosophy* since 1974. His latest book is *The Significance of Religious Experience*. Earlier he published two volumes in the philosophy of language, *The Magic Prism* and *Has Semantics Rested on a Mistake?*.

ABOUT THE AUTHOR

Gary Gutting is a distinguished academic philosopher and a major contributor to public discussions of philosophical questions.

He has taught for many years at the University of Notre Dame, where he holds the John A. O'Brien Chair in Philosophy. He is the author of seven academic books and editor of five others, and has published over forty articles. His main areas of research are philosophy of science, philosophy of religion, and twentieth-century French philosophy.

For a wider audience, he is the author of *Foucault: A Very Short Introduction*, a volume that has been translated into seven languages. Since 2011, he has been a regular contributor to the *New York Times* philosophy blog, *The Stone*, publishing over 100 columns and interviews.